THE FOUNTAIN

(FONS VITA

BY

SOLOMON IBN GABIROL

(Avicebron)

SPECIALLY ABRIDGED EDITION

TRANSLATED BY HARRY E. WEDECK

AZAFRAN BOOKS

Azafran Books, 2017

Published by Azafran Books –
http://www.azafranbooks.com/

The present translation is based on the Latin text edited by
Clemens Bäumker in *Beiträge zur Geshichte der Philosophie des
Mittelalters*, I. Münster, 1895. Volume Three of Ibn Gabirol's
work *Fons Vitae*.

ISBN-13: 978-0-9957279-5-3 (paperback)

First published in this edition: September 2017

Edited, formatted & design concept by Solomon James
Cover design & design concept by B.K.

Azafran Books
info@azafranbooks.com

CONTENTS

INTRODUCTION

The *Fons Vitae* of Solomon Ibn Gabirol (1021-1058/70) is essentially an eleventh century attempt to present the first part of wisdom as the source of life for the intellectually oriented Jews of the Western world. As such it suffered almost complete sterility right from the start. Written in Arabic, it seems to have by-passed the greater majority of Gabirol's own Jewish contemporaries. And, even when translated in the twelfth century into Latin by the combined efforts of Ibn Daud (Avendehut), who is better known by his assumed Christian name of John of Spain, and Dominic Gundissalin it was not immediately recognized as a work in medieval Jewish philosophy. This was probably due to the fact that the author of this work was designated by the Arabic form of his name: Avicebron. The florilegia selected and translated into Hebrew by Shem Tob Fahquera (1225-1290) made scant impression on his contemporaries, if we can judge from the fact that only one manuscript of it seems to have been circulated. Another fundamental reason for its lack of influence on the Jewish world may be the fact that Gabirol never betrays his Jewish commitments by the insertion of biblical phrases or references to the vast literature of Talmudic developments. Indeed, the neo-platonic linguistic structures and their somewhat Christian adaptations made his work appear positively non-Jewish. Abraham Ibn Daud (ca. 1110-1180) actually criticizes Gabirol for treating such an important topic that has so many religious implications, in a purely rationalistic way and, also, for expressing teachings apparently dangerous to Judaism itself. Later evaluations bring out the obvious lack of an appealing style, quite unexpected in a work by one recognized as pre-eminent in poetry.

The course of the *Fons Vitae* reached more fertile ground in the western Christian world of the thirteenth and fourteenth centuries. The very fact that Raymond, Archbishop of Toledo, had the translation prepared was some indication of the reception it was to get later. Its obvious neoplatonic orientation was welcomed by medieval schoolmen, already nourished by the speculations on universal hylomorphism derived from the writings of Augustine and elaborated within the Augustinian view of formlessness as the root distinction separating God and creatures. The wisdom of God and the wisdom of man meet quite amicably in the concept of a Will overflowing with light that enlightens every man that perfects every thing and illumines the path from the First Author, supreme and holy, to the least manifestation of reality, the substance supporting the nine categories. Though there appears to be in Gabirol a neo-platonic universe dependent on the Will of the First Agent, it is not quite appropriate to consider that Agent as Yahweh, in a truly Jewish sense. There are more Christian than Jewish delights savored in this treatise by the Christians of the thirteenth and fourteenth centuries.

After an introduction, in which the author explains that the *Fons Vitae* is the first part of wisdom or more accurately the first foundation and root of wisdom, he elaborates the steps to be followed from a knowledge of matter and form through the knowledge of will to the science of the First Essence. This is wisdom: to know the First Essence. The total universe of man's knowledge includes the "per se nota" and what can be proved by the rules of the dialectical art. Employing such rules he established the existence of matter and form, their combinations and implications. The cause of all things is the Prime Essence and Will is the medium between it and all these hylomorphically constituted things.

At first glance one may be apt to place Gabirol's understanding of matter and form in the Christian-Aristotelian tradition. Yet, on the surface, at least, there seem to be basic differences. One of these is the equation of the form of man with "the composition of his members" and another is the designation of body as a combination of matter, or hyle, and quantity in such a way that quantity is the first form, that is 'corporeitas.' Unlike Avicenna and later Christian universal hylomorphists he does not speak of a form of corporeity but only of a "matter of corporeity"; corporeity or quantity is the basic corporeal form. "Forma quantitatis cum coniungitur materiae inferiori constituit speciem corporis et eam ducit ad esse." (II. 8.) The composite corporeal substance is either the corporeal matter supporting the forms of qualities by means of quantity (Tract I) or spiritual matter which sustains the corporeal form (Tract II). Simple spiritual substances are shown to exist in the accompanying selection (Tract III); the way of understanding matter and form in simple substances (Tract IV) and universal matter and form (Tract V) rounds out the complete work.

There is a general method to be followed in this investigation: if you know that there are properties of something and know *what* they are, then you know the existence of the thing which has these properties. If there is one universal matter for all things it will have the following properties: it is "per se existens," "unius essentiae," "sustinens diversitatem," and "dans omnibus essentiam suam et nomen." Such properties are found in things and hence there is one universal matter. If you abstract all forms, sensible and intelligible, the remainder is universal matter. And the process is to go from color to figure, to corporeity, to substantiality, to "intellectus spirituales." Created being supporting all these forms is universal matter. The properties of universal form are: "subsistere in alio," "perficere essentiam illius in quo est," "dare ei esse."

The particular method is to inspect natural sensibles both universal and particular and you will find matter and form. To the four modes of matter: artificial-particular matter, natural-particular matter, natural-universal matter and celestial matter, there correspond four grades of forms. Sensible body is known or perceived by the sensible qualities adhering in it. This sensible body is understood in terms of substance when viewed with the forms; when conceived as receptive of these forms it is designated as matter or hyle. These sensible forms require an extended subject which is the body, composed of matter and corporeity (i.e., quantity). When the first form is added to the highest matter it constitutes the species of an intelligence. The form of the intelligence is a simple one whereas the form of quantity is many complex units. Of all forms, the former is the closest form to the highest matter, the latter is closest to the lowest matter. The form of the intelligence is not separated from the highest matter and quantity is not separated from the lowest. Each penetrates the total essence of its corresponding matter and supports all other appropriate forms.

It would be quite fascinating to conjecture about the antecedents of the basic ideas found in the *Fons Vitae*. With the sole exception of Plato there is no author mentioned by name throughout the whole five books. And even the references to Plato are quite vague and undeveloped. Because of certain anonymous references such as "it is said," "They have described," "why does one say," "I have often heard it said," "philosophers are accustomed to say," it may not be out of order to postulate that he considered his teaching within the generally accepted framework of Arabian-neo-platonism current at the time. Similar key ideas are found in the Karaitic writings of the tenth century under Mutazalite influences. He may be trying to reconcile the Arabian atomism and neoplatonic hylomorphism with a First Cause responsible for all because of Will, yet keeping that idea well within the Kalamite tradition. Such influences may have come through the Brethren of the Purity, who are generally conceded to have tried their hands at such typical neo-platonic attempts at unification. There are certain recognizable ideas of Avicenna, especially in regard to quantity and matter in itself. Though emanationism is a common neo-platonic explanation for the derivation of the many from the one, the intermediary of Will may be a somewhat later Sufi influence. Through the intermediary of Will, which is the divine power making matter and form and binding them together within the highest beings even down to the lowest, there flow from the First Essence the universal intelligence, souls, nature, the four elements and the particular corporeal beings of our experience.

The excerpt from the *Fons Vitae* presented here in English for the first time is taken from the third and middle tractate. Its primary purpose is to establish the existence of simple substances between the corporeal things of our experience and the First Agent or Author of all. Two methods are utilized: one is to consider the properties of the First Agent and the properties of the substance that supports the nine categories; the other is to examine the effects produced in the latter substance in accord with the general emanation of all from the First Author. The first really establishes the existence of simple substances; the second leads, synthetically and analytically, to a knowledge of what they are in themselves and how they are and why. Solomon Ibn Gabirol presents the complete integration of the simple substances into the overall pattern of universal hylomorphism. Here we have a very thorough cosmogony, cosmology, psychology and metaphysics.

Theodore E. James

DEMONSTRATION OF SIMPLE SUBSTANCES

Part I

Pupil: What is the problem that we are now to discuss in this book?

Master: Since it is our intention to find the matter and the form in simple substances, and since you question the existence of simple substances, we must first consider—and that is the purpose of this book—the proof of the existence of simple substances. We shall seek assured certainty in this regard to the point of establishing their existence by necessary proofs. Next we shall proceed to an examination of the science of matter and form in simple substances.

Let us begin then by producing the proofs that establish the existence of a substance intermediary between the First Author, sublime and holy, and the substance that supports the nine categories. In this connection we shall postulate the following fundamental principle: If the origin of beings is the First Author, who is not caused, and the end of beings is the final effect, that itself has no effect, then the beginning of things is essentially and actually different from their end. For if the beginning of things is not distinct from their end, then the beginning is the end, and the end is the beginning.

Pupil: What is the nature of the distinction between the First Author, sublime and holy, and the final effect?

Master: By the distinction between them, we understand the removal of resemblance and similitude; and with the removal of resemblance and similitude, union or harmony is removed, for there is harmony only through resemblance.

Pupil: How can it be asserted with truth that between the First Author and the substance that supports the nine categories there exist intermediary substances that are nearer to the First Author than this substance, while all things are distinct from him and none of them is more worthy of being near him than another?

Master: Why do you not set intermediary substances uninterruptedly after the First Author, holy and sublime, just as you placed the substance that supports the nine categories uninterruptedly after him; particularly when these substances are simple and spiritual?

Pupil: Proof of the existence of simple substances is very difficult. Demonstrate therefore the proofs that establish the existence of a substance intermediary between the First Author and the final effect.

Master: I shall expound for you various proofs of the existence of intermediary substances, each of which will prove the existence of simple substances. But I do not guarantee to demonstrate them in an order, because that would be of little value; and also you are to make an effort to arrange and join them properly one with the other. Remember then every term of their premises and observe the arrangements of terms in accordance with the rules of logic: then you will realize the truth of the conclusions that follow from these premises.

The First Author is the origin of all things. And the origin of things is different from their end. And the substance that supports the nine categories is the end of things. Therefore the First Author is different from the substance that supports the nine categories.

I shall now take this conclusion as a premise and I assert: The First Author differs from the substance that supports the nine categories. Now all different things have an intermediary. Therefore there is an intermediary between the First Author and the substance that supports the nine categories.

Pupil: What proof is there that there is an intermediary between all different things?

Master: If there were, between different things, no intermediary except themselves, they would then be a single thing and would not be different.

Pupil: Although the First Author is different from the substance that supports the nine categories, it is however not necessary that there should be an intermediary between them, for the soul is different from the body without an intermediary between them.

Master: But for the spirit that is intermediary between the soul and the body, they would not be united together. If then the First Author were different from the substance that supports the nine categories without any intermediary between them, they could not be united: and if they did not unite, the substance would not exist for a single instant.

Every substance is simple or compound. But everything simple is anterior to the compound because the simple is the cause of the compound. Now the substance that supports the nine categories is compound. Hence the simple substance is anterior to it.

Every compound is composed of its simple elements. But everything composed of its simple elements is posterior to the simple elements of which it is composed. Now the substance that supports the nine categories is composed of its simple elements. Hence this substance must be posterior to the simple elements of which it is composed.

The First Author is the true unity in whom there is no multiplicity; and the substance that supports the nine categories is the utmost multiplicity after which there is no greater multiplicity than itself. Now every compound multitude can be reduced to one. It is therefore necessary that there should be intermediaries between the true unity and the compound multitude.

It is necessary that the multitude that is in the substance that supports the nine categories should be subordinate to a unity belonging to the same genus as itself. Now the true unity is not of the same genus as itself. Therefore this multitude is not subordinate immediately to the true unity.

Every author makes only things that resemble him. Now the simple substance is like the First Author. Therefore the effect of the First Author is nothing but the simple substance.

The substance that supports the nine categories is multiple. Now everything multiple is an aggregate of numerous units. Therefore the substance that supports the nine categories is an aggregate of many units. What is less multiflex is always prior to every aggregate of many units. Therefore the other substance, which is of less complexity, is prior to the substance that supports the nine categories.

Before every aggregate that is the result of duplication, there must necessarily be multiples of two until numerical unity is reached. Now the substance that supports the nine categories is an aggregate resulting from duplication. Therefore there must be prior to it substances resulting from duplication, until one substance is reached.

The more a substance descends, the more it becomes multiple; and, on the other hand, the more it re-ascends, the more unified it becomes. Now whatever becomes multiple in declining and unified in rising necessarily reaches true unity. Therefore it is necessary that a multiple substance reach the substance truly unified.

The substance that supports the categories is a species with differences, properties, and accidents. Now every species differs from other species comprised in the same genus that it has in common with them. Therefore the substance that supports the categories differs from other species comprised in the same genus that it has in common with this species.

The order of the small world is the image of that of the great world. Now the substance of the intelligence, that is simpler and nobler than all the substances of the small world, is not conjoined to the body, for the soul and the spirit are intermediaries between them. And since the order of the great world is concluded from this, it follows that the simplest and most noble substance is not conjoined to the body, which is the substance that supports the categories.

If there is no intermediary between the First Author and the substance that supports the categories, it is necessary that the First Author should be the author of the substance by himself. Now if the First Author is the author by himself of the substance, this substance has always been with God. But this substance has not always been. Therefore it was not made by the essence of the First Author. Therefore the First Author is not the author by himself of the substance. And since the First Author is not its author by himself, there must necessarily be an intermediary between them. But if any one denies that there is an intermediary between them, the converse of this proposition must necessarily be true: that is, if there is no intermediary between the First Author and the substance that supports the categories, the Author is not the author by himself of the substance. But we have already declared that, if there is no intermediary between the First Author and the substance, he must necessarily be the author by himself. Hence he is not himself the author and he is at the same time the author: which is impossible.

It is necessary for the corporeal substance to move in a thing that comprises it and is conjoined to it. But the First Author does not comprise anything and is not conjoined to anything. Therefore the substance that has categories does not move in the First Author.

The motion of the substance that supports the categories exists in time. Now time falls under sempiternity. Therefore the substance that supports the categories falls under sempiternity. Now the First Author is above sempiternity. Therefore sempiternity is the intermediary between himself and substance. But sempiternity is sempiternity for an eternal thing and duration for a thing in duration. Therefore there is something intermediary between the First Author and the substance that supports the categories, whose eternity is duration. Therefore the substance that supports the categories is not conjoined to the First Author.

It is necessary that the power or the substance that moves the substance supporting the categories should be conjoined and mingled with it. Now the First Author is neither conjoined to anything nor mingled with it. Therefore the power or substance that moves the substance supporting the categories is not of the essence of the First Author. And since this power or substance does not belong to his essence, there must necessarily be another substance that is intermediary that gives motion to the substance that supports the categories.

Motion in place comes from the soul. But the substance that supports the categories moves by motion in place. Therefore the motion of this substance comes from the soul.

The act of the First Author is the creation of something from nothing. Now the substance that supports the categories is composed of its simple elements. Therefore it is not created from nothing.

Between two contrary terms there is always an intermediary that is similar to each term. But the First Author is contrary to the substance that supports the categories, for the First Author is the author only, while the substance that supports the categories is the effect only. Therefore there must necessarily be an intermediary between them that is both cause and effect.

To every being a different thing corresponds, that is its contrary. Now the substance that supports the categories is slow in motion, because its motion is in time. Therefore there must be another substance of greater velocity, whose motion is not in time; and this is the substance that is intermediary between the First Author and the substance that supports the categories.

The substance supporting the categories is of finite power; and this power comes either from the essence of the substance, or from elsewhere. But it is not possible that this power should come from the essence of the substance, since the substance is moved by another thing. And if this power does not come from the essence of the substance, it comes to it either from the essence of the First Author, or from an intermediary between them. But this power does not come from the essence of the First Author, for it would then be necessary for the essence of the First Author to be divided, since a finite power would come from it. But since an infinite thing is not divisible, the power that is in the substance supporting the categories cannot come from the essence of the First Author. Hence it was necessary that there should be another principle that is intermediary between them. And let no one object that the power of the intermediate substance is infinite: because, although the power of this substance is infinite according to its simplicity, yet it is finite because it is a created substance. It is therefore necessary for the intermediary substance to be finite, because it is created. Now its creator is infinite. Therefore, just as they differ in action and passion, so too they differ in being finite and infinite.

The substance supporting the categories is formed. Now every being formed is formed according to a model. Therefore the substance supporting the categories is formed according to a model. I shall now postulate this proposition and I shall assert: The substance supporting the categories is formed according to a model. Now in all cases where a thing is formed according to a model, the model is anterior to it. Therefore the model according to which the substance is formed is anterior to it. Now the model of a substance is a substance. Therefore the substance-model is anterior to the substance formed by it. Therefore a substance exists that is anterior to the substance supporting the categories.

Every substance intermediate between two substances touches them. Now the substance of the soul touches the substance of the intelligence and the substance supporting the categories is touched by it. Therefore the substance of the soul is intermediary between the substance of the intelligence and the substance supporting the categories.

Simple substances, like the soul and the intelligence, are forms of compound substances. But every form comprises the thing formed. Therefore simple substances comprise compound substances. Now the substance supporting the categories is compound. Therefore the simple substances comprise it. The higher a being is raised, the more it resembles the form. Therefore the superior must be the form of the inferior. Now the simple substance is superior to the compound substance. Therefore the simple substance is the form of the compound substance. Now the substance supporting the categories is compound. Therefore the simple substance is the form of the substance supporting the categories. The soul and the intelligence are simple substances. Now every simple substance comprises a compound substance. Therefore the soul and the intelligence comprise the substance supporting the categories. Now all that comprises another thing is superior to that which is comprised. Therefore the soul and the intelligence are superior to the substance supporting the categories.

The substance supporting the categories is a compound. Now between the compound and the simple there is no intermediary. Therefore there is no intermediary between the substance supporting the categories and the simple substance. Now whatever thing does not have an intermediary between itself and another thing, follows it in sequence. Therefore the substance supporting the categories follows the simple substance in sequence.

It is necessary that the First Author should accomplish his task beyond duration. Now when an author accomplishes his task beyond duration, it is necessary that what suffers his action without an intermediary should be accomplished in suffering it beyond duration. Therefore it is necessary that what suffers the action of the First Author without an intermediary should be accomplished in suffering it beyond duration. To this conclusion this minor premise is added: Now the substance supporting the categories is not accomplished beyond duration, for the motion of this substance is in time. It is therefore necessary that the substance supporting the categories should not suffer the action of the First Author without an intermediary.

It is necessary that every thing that suffers should suffer in action. Now all that suffers in action must necessarily receive the power of acting. Therefore it is necessary that all that suffers should receive the power of acting. After this conclusion, I postulate: It is necessary that what suffers immediately the action of the First Author should receive the power of acting. Now that which receives the power of acting, acts. Therefore it is necessary that what suffers immediately the action of the First Author, acts. And to this conclusion is added the following proposition: The substance supporting the categories does not act. Therefore this substance does not immediately suffer the action of the First Author.

The substance supporting the categories is mobile. Now everything mobile suffers. Therefore the substance with categories suffers. And every passion passes from potency to act. Therefore the passion of the substance supporting the categories passes from potency to act. I postulate this conclusion and say: The passion of the substance supporting the categories passes from potency to act. Now whenever a thing passes from potency to act, it is a being in action that attracts it into action. Therefore the passion of a substance supporting the categories attracts from potency to act only what exists in action without there being an intermediary between the substance and itself.

Similarly I take this conclusion as a premise and assert: The passion of the substance supporting the categories passes from potency to act by virtue of a being in action without there being an intermediary between them. Now the First Author is neither in power nor in action. Therefore the passion of the substance supporting the categories does not pass from power to act by virtue of the First Author without an intermediary between them.

The soul moves by itself beyond place. Now whatever is mobile by itself beyond place has a uniform motion. Therefore the soul moves by a uniform motion. I take this conclusion as a premise and I assert: The soul moves with a uniform motion. Now after every uniform motion comes a secondary thing. Therefore the uniform motion of the soul is followed by a secondary motion.

And according to another method: If the mind were by itself the first mobile, and the first motion were uniform, it is necessary that the motion of the soul should be a uniform motion. That the uniform motion is the first motion, is proved from this fact, that if uniform motion does not exist, secondary motion does not exist, nor the other motions. And as the soul in itself is the first mobile, it moves then with a uniform motion. I shall make this conclusion a premise and I assert: If the soul, which is in itself the first mobile, moves with a uniform motion, it is necessary that the mobile that follows move with a secondary motion. Therefore the mobile that follows moves with a secondary motion. But the soul, that is in itself the first mobile, moves with a uniform motion. Therefore the mobile that follows moves with a secondary motion. I shall treat this conclusion as a premise and I assert: The uniform motion of the soul is followed by a varied motion. Now the substance supporting the categories moves with a varied motion, for each part of this substance moves in two places only; because it moves from the first position to the second, from the second to the third: thus the second and the third are like the first and the second, and so on until the last of the positions. Since the uniform motion of the soul is followed by a secondary motion and the substance supporting the categories moves with a varied motion, the uniform motion of the soul is followed by the motion of the substance supporting the categories.

Similarly in another way: The substance supporting the categories moves with a secondary motion. Now all that moves with a secondary motion follows in sequence that which moves with a uniform motion. Hence the substances supporting the categories follow in sequence the substance that moves with a uniform motion. Likewise I take this proposition and I assert: The substance supporting the categories follows in sequence the substance that moves with a uniform motion. Now the soul moves with a uniform motion. Therefore the substance supporting the categories follows in sequence the substance of the soul.

Likewise in another way: If the secondary motion by which the substance that supports the categories is moved returns to the uniform motion, it is necessary that the motion of this substance should follow the uniform motion of the soul. But the secondary motion by which the substance that supports the categories is moved returns to the uniform motion, for each part of this mobile substance returns to the position from which it moved and then the motion of this substance is unified. Therefore the motion of the substance that supports the categories follows the uniform motion of the soul. Similarly I take this conclusion as a premise and I assert: If the motion of the substance that supports the categories follows the motion of the soul, it is necessary that the substance that supports the categories should follow the motion of the soul. Hence it is also necessary that the substance that supports the categories should follow the substance of the soul: that is, there is no intermediary between motion and substance. Now the motion of the substance that supports the categories follows the motion of the soul. Therefore it is necessary that the substance that supports the categories should follow the substance of the soul.

Whatever the being is that, in its entirety, receives something from another without an intermediary, it is more ready to receive it than if it received it with an intermediary. Therefore a whole that receives a thing without one of its parts receiving it more than another of its parts does, receives this thing that it receives without an intermediary more than with an intermediary.

The proof of this conclusion is demonstrated through the conversion of the negative proposition: whatever the whole is that receives something from another thing without an intermediary, there is no part of it that receives it more than another of its parts does. And the converse of this proposition is as follows: Whatever the whole is that receives a thing without one of its parts receiving it more than another of its parts, it receives it without an intermediary. To this proposition we add the following universal affirmative: A whole that receives something from another thing without an intermediary receives it more than if it received it with an intermediary. Therefore whatever the being that receives something without one of its parts receiving it more than another of its parts, it receives it more without an intermediary than if it received it with an intermediary.

Then we shall pose this affirmative: A substance is so constituted that one of its parts receives more motion than another. I shall add a negative and the following syllogism appears: A substance is so constituted that one of its parts receives the form more than another. Now a whole that receives something without one of its parts receiving it more than another, receives it more than if it received it with an intermediary. Therefore the substance does not receive the form more than if it received it with an intermediary.

Next we shall propose this universal: Whatever receives something without an intermediary receives it more than if it received it with an intermediary. To this I add the negative: A substance does not receive the form more than if it received it with an intermediary: and the following syllogism arises: Whatever receives something without an intermediary receives it more than if it received it with an intermediary. Now a substance does not receive the form more than if it received it with an intermediary. Therefore the substance does not receive the form without an intermediary.

The proof of this conclusion is demonstrated by the conversion of the following affirmative proposition: Whatever receives something without an intermediary receives it more than if it received it with an intermediary. The converse of this proposition is as follows: Whatever receives something without an intermediary more than with an intermediary receives it without an intermediary. The following syllogism takes places: The substance does not receive the form more than if it received it with an intermediary. Now whatever receives something without an intermediary more than with an intermediary receives it without an intermediary. Therefore the substance does not receive the form without an intermediary.

Similarly in another way. The substance that supports the categories is so constituted that one of its parts receives the form more than another. Now a whole that receives something and a part of which receives it more than another of its parts does not receive this thing without some intermediary. Therefore the substance that supports the categories has no form without some intermediary.

If all beings have their contraries and if the substance that supports the categories is a force that receives its own form, it is necessary that there should be a force contrary to it that receives all forms. And this is the property of simple substances.

If the common root of beings is constituted in contrary terms, it is necessary that all beings comprised in this root should constitute contrary terms. Now the root of beings is constituted of contrary terms, for it bears and is borne. It is therefore necessary that all beings dependent on this root should constitute contrary terms.

If there exists a compound substance, it is necessary that there should exist a simple substance contrary to it. Now the compound substance exists. Therefore the simple substance also exists. And if the simple substance exists, it is either above the compound substance or below it. If the simple substance is below the compound substance, then the simple substance is created by the compound substance. But the compound substance is created by the simple substance. Therefore the simple substance is not below the compound substance. And since it is not below it, it must necessarily be above it. Hence the following syllogism: A simple substance is above a compound substance. Now the substance that supports the categories is compound. Therefore a simple substance is above a substance that supports the categories.

A simple substance and a compound substance are united without loss of any of their forms. Now all things that are united without loss of any of their forms are in harmony. Therefore the simple substance and the compound substance are in harmony. And all things that are in agreement are of the same genus. Therefore the simple substance and the compound substance are of the same genus. Now all things that are of the same genus fall under what is their genus. Therefore the simple substance and the compound substance fall under the same genus. Therefore there is a substance above them, more simple than they and common to them.

If the First Author is the author beyond time, it is necessary that the first being to suffer his action should suffer it beyond time. But the First Author acts beyond time. Therefore the first being to suffer his action must suffer it beyond time. I take this conclusion and I assert: It is necessary that the first being to suffer his action should suffer it beyond time. Now the substance that supports the categories does not suffer beyond time. Therefore the substance that supports the categories is not the first object of the action of the First Author. It is necessary that everything that suffers should suffer in time or beyond time. Let us first postulate the following principle: Everything that suffers beyond time is anterior to that which suffers in time. And let us take the converse to this proposition: All that is anterior to that which suffers in time itself suffers beyond time. And we shall add this minor premise: Whenever a being suffers beyond time, there does not exist anything else that suffers anterior to it. Therefore whenever a being is anterior to that which suffers in time, there exists no other sufferer anterior to it.

Let us postulate this second principle: All that suffers in time, is posterior to that which suffers beyond time. Let us take the converse of this proposition, namely: All that is posterior to that which suffers beyond time, suffers in time. And let us add this second proposition: Whenever a thing suffers in time, there exists no other sufferer posterior to it. Therefore after that which is posterior to that which suffers beyond time, there exists no other sufferer posterior to it.

And to this conclusion we shall add another proposition: The substance that supports the categories suffers in time. And all that suffers in time is posterior to that which suffers beyond time. Therefore the substance that supports the categories is posterior to that which suffers beyond time. And to this conclusion I shall add the first conclusion: Whenever a being is posterior to that which suffers beyond time, there does not exist another sufferer posterior to it. Therefore after the substance that supports the categories there does not exist any other sufferer.

Similarly in another way and in a concise manner: A simple substance suffers beyond time, and a compound substance suffers in time. But there is no other being that suffers anterior to that which suffers beyond time, and there is no other being that suffers posterior to that which suffers in time. Therefore there does not exist any other being that suffers anterior to the simple substance; nor any other being that suffers posterior to the compound substance that supports the categories.

All that moves perpetually with a local motion is separated from the past motion and is prepared for the future motion. Now all that is separated from one thing and approaches another, passes from potency to act. Similarly I shall say next: The substance that supports the categories moves perpetually with a local motion. Now all that moves perpetually with a local motion proceeds from potentiality to act. Therefore the substance that supports the categories proceeds from potentiality to act. Now all that proceeds from potentiality to act is not perfect. Therefore the substance that supports the categories is not perfect. I shall then say: If some author is perfect, the immediate object of his action is perfect. But the First Author is perfect. Therefore the immediate object of his action is perfect. I take this conclusion as a premise and say: The immediate object of the action of the First Author is perfect. But the substance that supports the categories is not perfect. Therefore the substance that supports the categories is not the immediate object of the action of the First Author.

The forms subsisting in the substance that supports the categories proceed from potentiality to act. Now whatever passes somewhere from potentiality to act draws along nothing except that which exists in act, and the first thing is the second in potentiality. Therefore the forms subsisting in the substance that supports the categories pass from potentiality to act only through other forms that exist in act, and the first forms are the second in potentiality. Let us take this conclusion as a premise, and add the following proposition: The essence of the First Author has no form. Therefore the forms subsisting in the substance that supports the categories do not pass from potentiality to act by the essence of the First Author.

Whenever anything receives something from another without an intermediary, nothing more worthy than it can be found to receive this thing. If the substance that supports the categories receives substantiality from the First Author without an intermediary, then no other substance can be found more worthy than it of the name of substance. But the simple substance, like the soul and the intelligence, is more worthy of the name of substance than the substance that supports the categories. Therefore the substance that supports the categories does not receive substantiality immediately from the First Author.

The principle that moves without an intermediary the substance that supports the categories cannot be infinite for it must necessarily move it either of itself or by accident. And if it moves it by its essence, and its essence is infinite, it is not possible for the motion that proceeds from it to be finite. Now the motion of the substance is finite. Therefore the essence that moves it is not infinite. And if it moves it by accident, its essence is not infinite either, for all that is infinite does not receive any accident. And the proof of this is as follows: A thing that is infinite does not change. Now everything that receives accidents changes. Therefore an infinite thing does not receive any accident.

Therefore it is not possible for the immediate mover of the substance to be infinite. Therefore it is finite. We take this conclusion and assert: The immediate mover of the substance with categories is finite. Now the First Author is infinite. Therefore the First Author is not the immediate mover of the substance.

Part II

Similarly, in another way, if the immediate mover of the substance is infinite, the motion of the substance is infinite. But it is impossible for the motion of the substance to be infinite, since its substance is finite. Therefore it is impossible for the immediate mover of this substance to be infinite. Next we shall add to this conclusion the following proposition: The First Author is infinite. Therefore it is impossible for the First Author to be the immediate mover of the substance.

The motion of the substance that supports the categories cannot but be either natural or voluntary. If it is natural, the First Author is not its immediate mover, for the First Author does not cause a natural effect without an intermediary. And if it is voluntary, and the substance in itself has no will, it is necessary for the substance to depend on another substance that gives it a will to move. Now it is impossible that this substance should be the First Author, for the First Author is not mobile. Therefore this substance that gives motion to the substance that supports the categories is different from the First Author. Therefore the First Author is not the immediate mover of the substance.

The substance that moves the substance supporting the categories must be either mobile or immobile. If it is immobile, it cannot move the substance that supports the categories, for this substance either can move or cannot. If it can move, it would be mobile. If it cannot move in itself, it could not possibly move another thing.

The proof of the impossibility for the mover of the substance to be able to move it, since it cannot move itself, is as follows: Let us assume that that which moves the substance cannot move itself. Now everything that cannot move itself cannot move anything else. Therefore what we have assumed as the mover of the substance cannot move it. Therefore it is impossible for the mover of the substance to move it and not be mobile in itself. Therefore the mover of the substance is mobile.

And the proof that the mover of the substance that gives the substance the faculty of moving is mobile is demonstrated thus: The mover of the substance gives the substance the faculty of moving. Now whatever gives a thing to another thing is more worthy of possessing the thing given than that which receives it. Therefore the mover of the substance that gives the substance the faculty of moving is more worthy of possessing the faculty of moving than the substance that receives it. Therefore the immediate mover of the substance is mobile. I take this conclusion and assert: The substance that moves the substance without an intermediary is mobile. Now the First Author is not mobile. Therefore the First Author is not the immediate mover of the substance.

The substance that supports the categories is a body. Now every body in itself is at rest. Therefore the substance that supports the categories in itself is at rest. Now everything that is at rest depends on a mobile end. Therefore the substance that supports the categories depends on a mobile end. Now all that depends on a mobile end has a mobile anterior to it. Therefore the substance that supports the categories has a mobile anterior to it. But everything mobile is substance. Therefore the substance that supports the categories has another mobile substance anterior to it.

The substance that is the object of the action by the First Author must be either mobile or immobile. Now it is impossible for it not to be mobile, for the First Author is a mover; and if the object of his action were not mobile, he himself would not be a mover. It is therefore necessary for the object of the action by the First Author to be mobile.

Hence it moves either in time or beyond time. Now it is impossible that it should be mobile in time, for its mover is a mover beyond time. This is the form of the argument: The first mover moves beyond time. Now what is moved by a mover beyond time is moved beyond time. Therefore that which is moved by the first mover moves beyond time. Now the substance that supports the categories does not move beyond time. Therefore the substance that supports the categories is not moved by the first mover.

It is necessary that if there exists something that moves in time, there should exist also something beyond time, for if nothing moved beyond time, the first mover would not be a mover beyond time, but he would move in time. Therefore the first mover would move in time and at the same time would move beyond time: which is impossible.

If the First Author is not mobile, it is necessary that the substance that he moves should be mobile beyond time, because if the substance were mobile in time, it would be necessary that there should exist anterior to it a mobile beyond time. But there is nothing anterior to it except the first mover. Therefore the first mover would move beyond time. But the first mover is not mobile in any manner. Therefore the substance that he moves does not move in time. Now we take this proposition and we assert: That which is moved by the first mover does not move in time. Now the substance that supports the categories moves in time. Therefore that which is moved by the first mover is not the substance that supports the categories.

The motion that is in the substance that supports the categories is variable. Now everything variable is passive. Therefore the motion that is in the substance that supports the categories is passive. But the essence of the First Author is not passive. Therefore the motion that is in the substance supporting the categories does not come from the essence of the First Author. Therefore it comes from the essence of another substance.

Everything by means of which something that is moved is passive will have a passive essence. Now the motion that is in the substance supporting the categories is passive. Therefore the substance that causes its motion is passive. Similarly, I assert: The substance that causes the motion of the substance supporting the categories is passive. Now the First Author is not passive. Therefore the First Author does not cause the motion of the substance supporting the categories.

The diffused motion in the substance supporting the categories must be either a substance or an accident. If it is an accident, its author is a substance; and this substance is either finite or infinite. Now it is impossible that it should be infinite, for it is conjoined to a finite substance. But if it is finite, it is not the First Author.

And if the motion is a substance, what is proper to the creative substance is proper to it that is finiteness or infinitude. If it is finite, it is impossible that it should be the First Author. And if it is infinite, it cannot unite with a finite substance and cannot produce a finite work. Now the moving substance is united to a finite substance and produces a finite work, for all the motions that are found in the substance are finite. Therefore the substance that moves the substance supporting the categories is not infinite. Now the First Author is infinite. Therefore the substance that moves the substance supporting the categories is not the First Author.

All that moves in an infinite place cannot possibly traverse this place in a finite time. The substance that supports the categories traverses the place in which it moves in a finite time. Therefore the substance supporting the categories cannot possibly move in an infinite place. Then I postulate this proposition and assert: The substance supporting the categories does not move in an infinite place. Now the First Author is an infinite place. Therefore the substance supporting the categories does not move in the First Author.

Similarly, in another way, the substance that supports the categories traverses the place in which it moves in a finite time. Now whenever a thing traverses the place in which it moves in a finite time, the place in which it moves is finite. Therefore the place in which the substance supporting the categories moves is finite. And when we add to this conclusion the affirmation that the First Author is not finite, the conclusion is that the place in which the substance that supports the categories moves is not the First Author.

The substance that supports the categories is finite. Now a finite substance cannot move in an infinite substance. Therefore the substance that supports the categories cannot possibly move in an infinite substance. To this conclusion I shall add this proposition: The First Author is infinite. Therefore the substance that supports the categories cannot possibly move in the First Author.

Every simple substance that unites by itself with another substance is finite; being terminated where it unites with the other substance. Now whenever a thing is terminated in another thing, its essence is finite. Therefore every simple substance that unites with another substance has a finite essence. I now take this proposition and assert as follows: Every simple substance that unites by itself with another substance has a finite essence. Now the essence of the First Author is infinite. Therefore the essence of the First Author is not united with any one of the simple finite substances. Similarly I take this conclusion and add the following proposition: The essence of the substance that supports the categories is finite. Therefore the essence of the First Author is not united to the substance that supports the categories. If between the essence of the First Author and the substance that supports the categories there were no intermediary, the essence of the First Author would be united to the substance that supports the categories. But the essence of the First Author is not united to the substance that supports the categories. Therefore between the essence of the First Author and the substance that supports the categories there is an intermediary.

Everything that is simple or compound and finite in essence is united to another thing only by its extremity. Now whenever a thing unites with another by its extremity, inversely the other thing unites with the first thing by its extremity. Therefore whenever a thing is of finite essence, whatever unites with it is finite; and everything that follows the finite that unites with it is of finite essence. Now the substance that supports the categories is of finite essence. Therefore the substance that follows it is of finite essence.

If the substance that supports the categories is created independently of another thing, there exists nothing else more perfect and stronger than it. Now there exists a substance more perfect and stronger than this one. Therefore this substance is not created independently by another thing.

Similarly, in another way, if there exists a substance more perfect than the substance supporting the categories, then the substance supporting the categories proceeds from it. All that proceeds from another thing is posterior to the power from which it proceeds; and all that is posterior to some power is not so perfect as the principle of the power from which it proceeds. Therefore everything that proceeds from another thing is not so perfect as the principle of that from which it proceeds. Then I take this proposition and assert: All that proceeds from something else is not so perfect as the principle of that from which it proceeds. Now all that is not so perfect as the principle of that from which it proceeds is imperfect. Therefore all that proceeds from something else is imperfect. Similarly I take this proposition and assert: All that proceeds from something else is imperfect. Now to everything imperfect corresponds something more perfect. Therefore to everything that proceeds from something else corresponds something else more perfect than it.

Next I shall take the converse of this proposition: Everything to which a more perfect thing corresponds proceeds from something else. To this we add the following proposition: There exists another substance more perfect than the substance that supports the categories. Therefore the substance that supports the categories proceeds from something else. Similarly, from this point on: The substance that supports the categories proceeds from something else. Now all that proceeds from something else is of the same genus as that from which it proceeds. Therefore the substance that supports the categories is of the same genus as that from which it proceeds. Similarly from this point on: The substance that supports the categories is of the same genus as that from which it proceeds. Now the substance that supports the categories is a substance. Therefore that from which it proceeds is also a substance. Therefore this is the substance superior to the substance that supports the categories from which it proceeds.

The substance of the intelligence has every form. Now everything that has every form must be anterior to that which has only some forms and is more subtle than it. Therefore the substance of the intelligence is anterior to that which has only some forms and is more subtle than it. Then to this conclusion I shall add this proposition: The substance that supports the categories has some forms only. Therefore the substance of the intelligence is anterior to the substance that supports the categories and is more subtle than it.

The substance of intelligence suffers beyond time. Now everything that suffers beyond time is anterior to that which suffers in time and is more subtle than it. Therefore the substance of the intelligence is prior to that which suffers in time and is more subtle than it. To this conclusion I add the following proposition: The substance that supports the categories suffers in time. Therefore the substance of the intelligence is anterior to the substance that supports the categories and is more subtle than it.

If there existed a substance anterior to the substance that supports the categories and more subtle than it, the substance that supports the categories would not be the immediate object of the action of the First Author. But the substance of the intelligence is anterior to the substance that supports the categories and more subtle than it. Therefore the substance that supports the categories is not the immediate object of the action of the First Author. And the converse of this proposition: If the substance that supports the categories is the immediate object of the action of the First Author, there is no other substance more subtle than it and anterior to it. But the substance of the intelligence is anterior to it and is more subtle than it. Therefore it is not the immediate object of the action of the First Author.

The form that subsists in the substance that supports the categories is in it accidentally. Now what is in something accidentally is essentially in its cause. Therefore the form that subsists in the substance that supports the categories accidentally is essentially in its cause. Then I take this proposition and I assert: The form borne accidentally by the substance that supports the categories is essentially in its cause. Now whatever is essentially in its cause is a proper accident for its cause. Therefore the form borne by the substance that supports the categories is a proper accident for its cause. Then I take this proposition and I add another: There is no accident in the essence of the First Author. Therefore the form borne by the substance that supports the categories is not in the essence of the First Author. Then I take this proposition and I assert: The form borne by the substance that supports the categories is essentially in its cause. Therefore the First Author is not the essential cause of the form. Therefore there is another substance that is the essential cause of this form, and this form has existence in this substance through creation by the First Author.

The First Author is the origin of things. Now whatever is the origin of things has as a contrary the extremity of things. Therefore the First Author has an extremity that is contrary to him. Then I take this proposition and I add: The substance that supports the categories is the extremity of things. Therefore the substance that supports the categories is the extremity that is opposed to the First Author. Then I take this proposition and I add: Whenever there is a last term for a first term, there is an intermediary between them. Therefore between the substance that supports the categories and the First Author there is an intermediary.

Whatever begins to exist, before existence, is possible of existence. Now whatever is possible before existence is necessary after having been possible. Then I take this proposition and I assert: Whatever is possible before it existed is necessary after having been possible. Now whatever is necessary after having been possible has now passed from possibility to necessity. Therefore whatever is possible after not having existed has now passed from possibility to necessity. From this conclusion we draw what it has in potentiality and we say: The possibility of being that which did not exist changes into necessity. Now whatever changes into something is of the same genus as the thing into which it changes. Therefore the possibility is of the same genus as the necessity.

Next we assume the following observation and we assert: The substance that supports the categories presents in place parts that were not there previously; it is found to be draped in some form in which it had not previously been draped. Now whatever is after not having been, was possible. Therefore the substance supporting the categories is said to be possible. Similarly: The substance supporting the categories is said to be possible. Now all that is defined as possible must necessarily have something anterior to it that is defined by necessity, for necessity is anterior to possibility. Therefore the substance supporting the categories defined as possible must have anterior to it something defined by necessity. Similarly I take this proposition as a premise: The substance supporting the categories defined as possible must have anterior to it something that is defined by necessity. Now the possible and the necessary are of the same genus, as has been stated. Therefore the substance supporting the categories is of the same genus as the substance anterior to it.

Similarly, in another way: The necessary substance is anterior to the possible substance. Now the substance that supports the categories is possible. Therefore the necessary substance is anterior to the substance that supports the categories. Similarly: The necessary substance is anterior to the substance that supports the categories. The necessary substance is of the same genus as the possible substance. Therefore the substance anterior to the substance supporting the categories is of the same genus as the possible substance. Now the substance supporting the categories is possible. Therefore the substance that is anterior to the substance supporting the categories is of the same genus as it.

We have now advanced all that it was possible to advance regarding the proofs to demonstrate that the substance supporting the categories is not moved by the First Author without an intermediary; and it is clear that there exists another substance intermediary between the First Author and the substance supporting the categories.

Pupil: Certainly the proofs that you have adduced are an excellent demonstration for me. But I should like you to summarize what you have already said on this subject and to postulate a general rule relating to the investigation of the existence of the substance intermediary between the First Author and the substance that supports the categories.

Master: You must know that the substance intermediary between the First Author and the substance supporting the categories is not one substance, but many. Now we can investigate in two ways the existence of those substances that are intermediary between the First Author and the substance that supports the categories. One of these ways is to consider the properties of the First Author and the properties of the substance that supports the categories; and it was according to this method that we established all the proofs that we have adduced up to this point. The second method is based on an investigation of the existence of the substances intermediary between the First Author and the substance that supports the categories according to the effects and actions of these substances and according to the emanation of their powers from each other. I call actions and effects of these substances the figures that appear in the substance that supports the categories and which it receives from the action on it of the simple substances, and the passions that, in each of the simple substances, are the effects of these substances upon each other. The difference in these methods consists in this, that the first leads us to the knowledge of the absolute existence of the substance intermediary between the First Author and the substance that supports the categories. The second method leads us to a knowledge of what the intermediary substance is, how it is, and why it is.

Pupil: I should like to be convinced of the truth of the proofs that we have established by the first method before we undertake to establish the proofs by the second method. And I ask you to remove the doubt that I have on this matter; for I know that all the terms of the propositions advanced in the proofs are defined, for it is necessary that there should be either genera, or species, or differences, or individuals, or properties or accidents; I know also none of these things applies to the First Author. How then can the proofs that you have adduced be true?

Master: Our intention in regard to the definition of the terms of the propositions advanced in the proofs was merely to know the terms, and now we have in some manner a knowledge of the First Author according to his properties, although he is not defined. Therefore there was no need for us, since we know something of him, to treat of the definition of the terms of the proposition adduced in the proofs in regard to him. But the definitions that are predicated from the terms of these proofs are taken either from the properties of the essence of the First Author, or from the effects that are attributed to him, or from the properties of those things that are inferior to him and that are not attributed to him. When we describe him by properties that are said to be his, what is achieved thus is an affirmative proposition. And when we take away from him some property not attributed to him, what is thus achieved is a negative proposition, and it will constitute in the proofs a true proposition.

If both propositions adduced in the syllogisms are theological, their affirmative and negative connection will depend on the affirmative and negative connection of the two terms of each of the propositions.

And if one proposition is theological and the other not, their negative connection depends on the two terms of the negative theological premise—negative, I assert, that is by taking away from God the blessed, the non-divine property; and their connection cannot be affirmative, since it is impossible for God to be described by a non-theological property.

Pupil: What your words imply is that the propositions are of two kinds: divine and not divine. But I doubt whether the divine proof is a proof, since it contains neither genus nor species nor any of the logical terms.

Master: Since you are convinced of the connection of the terms of the theological propositions, although the case is not the same as in the case of the non-divine proposition, yet each of the propositions is similar to the other in order and arrangement, that is, in the position of the terms considered according to the rules of the logical figures.

It is therefore not inappropriate, it is even necessary, that it should be called a divine proof, since the non-divine proof is the conjunction of true propositions and their arrangement according to the rules of the logical figures, and the divine proof is similar to it. Also, the propositions adduced in the divine proof are either first or second. If they are first, then they will be equal to the first propositions that are adduced in the non-divine proof. If they are second, they must have been drawn from the source of the second propositions advanced in the non-divine proof; and since this is so, they are equal to them. Therefore the divine proof and the non-divine proof, in so far as their truth is involved, are equal. And since this is the case, it is not inadmissible, it is even necessary that the divine proof should be called a proof.

Pupil: Why did the one who said this say that in divine knowledge there is no proof?

Master: The one who said this, if he meant that in divine knowledge there is no proof whatever, was wrong. If he meant that in divine knowledge we do not use the non-divine proof that is composed of logical terms, he was right, and I do not contradict him.

Pupil: Now I know clearly the existence of the intermediary between the First Author and the substance that supports the categories according to the method of considering the properties of the First Author and the properties of the substance that supports the categories. This is evident to me from the proofs that you have presented according to this method. Thanks to them the doubt that I entertained is gone and it is now evident to me that they are true. Show me now the existence of the substance intermediary between the First Author and the substance that supports the categories, according to the effects and the results and according to the emanation.

Master: Do you consider it necessary or not to grant the actions of things upon each other?

Pupil: Why should I not grant it, when the evidence of the thing and due reflection demonstrate the existence of these actions? But I do not know what this action is, or why it is, or how it is.

Master: What the action is, is this; that a thing gives its form to another thing when both things are apt for this. Now as to how, there is either a conjunction without an intermediary, or a conjunction with an intermediary, or there is a change and diminution of the form of the agent; or, on the contrary, there is no diminution of the quality of the agent; or there is an impression of the power of the agent upon the passive thing beyond time; or there is an opinion or an imagination, like the action of a loved object on the lover. But as to why there is this action of things upon each other, this occurs through the sublime universal cause, because the power that is the author of all things and moves all things by itself operates as long as it finds something to receive its action.

Hence it is necessary that the universal form, made by this power, should also act by itself. It is therefore a maker and an agent. Similarly it is also necessary that the first universal matter should receive the action by itself. Now it is the property of the universals that their nature should be in their parts. And since the parts receive their nature from the essence of the universals, they also give it to themselves. It is therefore necessary that they should receive it from their universals. And it is consequently necessary that all forms should be active and all matters passive. In regard to the form, the argument is as follows: The universal form acts necessarily. Now whenever a universal thing acts necessarily, its parts act necessarily. Therefore the parts of the universal form act necessarily. The argument for matter is as follows: The universal matter receives the action of the form. Whenever a universal thing receives the action of the form, all its parts receive it also. Therefore all the parts of the universal matter receive the action of the form.

Pupil: Why is the universal form said to act necessarily?

Master: Because the First Author, sublime and holy, dispenses the abundance that he has with him, for all that exists flows from him. And since the First Author is the dispenser of the form that is with him, he does not prevent it from flowing out; he is therefore the source that maintains, envelops, and comprehends everything that is. Hence it is necessary that all substances should obey his action and imitate him in giving their forms and bestowing their energies, as long as they find a matter ready to receive them. Now by the emanation of substances is understood their motion and desire to communicate the action, wherein they imitate the First Author.

But they differ in this according to their perfection and imperfection, for some of them flow beyond time, and others in time; and the different superior substances, in the emanation of their flow, are in relation to the inferior substances just as the First Author is to the superior and inferior substances in regard to his emanation over them, although their flow is different in each case. Similarly the superior substances are in relation to the First

Author, in their passivity in regard to him, just like the inferior substances in relation to the superior substances in their passivity in regard to them. In short, the first emanation, that embraces all substances, makes it necessary that the substances emanate into others. And in this regard take an example from the sun that does not emanate by itself and does not communicate its rays except for the reason that it falls under the first emanation and obeys it.

When we study the cause of the emanation of substances from each other, we shall find still other causes for this phenomenon. One of these is that the form is more subtle than the matter. And since the subtle penetrates and traverses that which is before it and opposes it, it follows necessarily that the form penetrates and traverses all that is before it and opposes it.

Furthermore, it is the nature of the form to unite with the matter, when the matter is ready to receive it. Now all that unites with something that is ready to receive it gives itself to this thing and also gives it its form. It is therefore necessary that the form should give itself and its form to that which is prepared to receive it. And this is a very evident proof that the form proceeds from the First Author and obeys him, because it is forced by its nature to give itself and to give its form when it finds a matter to receive it. Furthermore, because there was a first effect and a first action, it was necessary that this effect and this action should penetrate everything until there was nothing left to receive them.

Pupil: Now I know what action is, how it is, and why it is. Now show me also how many passive things there are.

Master: Since the active thing is either matter or form, its action must be similar either to itself and the form, or to the form only; and the form must be either a force, or a corporeal form, or a motion. Since this is the case, know that the passive thing is either a formed essence or a force, or a corporeal form, or a motion.

Pupil: I now know from what has preceded that everything that has a form acts by itself and its species, when it finds a matter to receive it.

Master: If there are simple substances apart from the substance that supports the categories, is it not necessary that they should act by themselves and their forms?

Pupil: Yes: since we have discovered that things communicate their energies and their lights, it is necessary also that simple substances should do so.

Master: Furthermore, it is necessary that the essences and the forms of these substances communicate with each other more than those of other substances, on account of their force and subtlety and their light. For we find that the more the substance is subtle, strong, and luminous, the stronger its action will be, and the more capable to penetrate into another substance beyond time.

Pupil: What proof of this is there?

Master: The emanation comes from the impulsion: and the impulsion comes from the force. The proof that the force and the subtlety cause the emanation is that the quantity and the figure do not imprint their image on what is before them, when it can receive it; and this on account of the weakness of the quantity and its thickness for penetration. Similarly with the accident, for the stronger, more subtle, and more luminous it is, the more penetrating it is. We conclude therefore from these six proofs that it is necessary that the simple substances should give themselves and communicate their forms. Further, the fact that the energies and the rays that emanate from the body are spiritual is a proof that the spiritual substance must also emanate. Further, although we have found that the corporeal substance is prevented from communicating itself on account of the thickness of the quantity and its obscurity, yet the quantity communicates its shadow to the bodies that are before it, so that, when it meets a luminous body, it gives it its form: all the more necessary, according to this consideration, is it that the spiritual substance, which is exempt from quantity, should emanate its essence and its force and its light.

Pupil: How well you have proved the active and penetrating character of simple substances!

Master: The more subtle, the stronger and better they are, the more apt they are to act and to communicate themselves with what they have. This is evident from the absence of the penetrating power in the corporeal substances, for when you consider these substances one after the other, some are the testimony and the proof of the others. For when you postulate that the corporeal substance is prevented from communicating itself on account of its thickness and its obscurity, and that the more remote it is from thickness and obscurity, the nearer it is to communicating itself, you necessarily assume thereby that the simple substances communicate themselves, their energies and forms.

For, since the quantity prevents the substance from communicating itself, there is nothing that prevents the spiritual substances from giving their forms and bestowing their energies. And when you assume that the simple substances communicate themselves and their forms, you necessarily assume that the corporeal substances are prevented from communicating themselves and their forms. And when you observe that the essence of the simple substance has no end, when you consider its force, when you think of its faculty of penetrating into a thing that is before it and that is prepared to receive it, when you compare it with the corporeal substance, you will find that the corporeal substance is powerless to be everywhere and too feeble to penetrate things; and you will find that the simple substance, the substance of the universal soul, is diffused through the entire universe and that it sustains it in itself on account of its subtlety and simplicity: and you will find similarly that the substance of the universal intelligence is diffused through the entire universe and that it penetrates it. The cause of this is the subtlety of the two substances, their force and their light: and on account of this the substance of the intelligence is diffused into the interior of things and penetrates them. Therefore according to this view all the more ought the power of the holy God to penetrate all things, exist in all things, and act in all things beyond time.

Pupil: Now it is clear to me that every simple substance communicates itself and gives its form. But what follows from this?

Master: From this it follows that the simple substances communicate themselves and give their forms to the substance that supports the categories, for each spiritual substance causes through itself, as we have said, its proper effect on the thing that is before it, and that because it emanates and dominates all substances when it finds a subject to receive its action. For this reason, it is necessary that the simple substance that follows the compound substance should cause in the compound substance what it must cause. And because this substance is a sensible compound body, it necessarily follows that the action of the spiritual substance in this body should be sensible also: except that this action is not corporeal absolutely nor spiritual absolutely, but is intermediary between the two extremes, like the growth and the sensibility, the motion, and the colors and the figures that are in the compound substances the effects of the simple substances. For these effects are not corporeal absolutely nor spiritual absolutely, since they are perceived by the senses.

Therefore, according to what we have said, all the sensible forms in the corporeal substance must come from the action of the intelligible spiritual substance. And these forms are sensible only because the matter that receives them is very close by its nature to corporeality; and these sensible forms exist in the intelligible spiritual substance more simply than in the matter.

An example of this is the emanation or the issuance of the form from the simple spiritual substance and of its action in the corporeal matter, like the light of the sun, that is diffused in the air, penetrates it and yet does not appear visible on account of the subtlety of the air, until it meets a solid body, like the earth: then the light becomes sensible because it cannot penetrate the parts of this body and be diffused through them, but stops on the surface of the body, and its essence is concentrated so that its emanation becomes brighter. In a similar manner the lights of the simple substances penetrate and flow through each other without the perception of the senses, on account of the subtlety and the simplicity of these substances. But when the lights penetrate to the corporeal matter, then the light becomes visible and is revealed to the senses on account of the thickness of the corporeal matter.

And in this manner we rise to the concept that every form borne by the universal matter exists in the essence of the power that gives it, that is, in the essence of the will, more simply than in the essence of the first matter that receives it. And as the first matter differs by its nature from the essence of the will and resembles the body in relation to the will, it is necessary that the action of the will in the matter should be perceptible, as the action of the intelligible substances is perceptible in the body. It is also necessary that the will should extrude what it has in its essence and give it to the matter, just as the intelligible substances effect the extrusion of what they have in their essence and give it to the body: except that the will acts beyond time, without motion, without organ, and beyond space, while the intelligible substances do the very opposite. That is why the simple substances and in general all the substances in all their actions act according to the first action that moves and penetrates everything. And in this way we shall realize the diffusion of the first power and of the first action in all beings, for the energies of the simple substances, and in general the energies of all beings spread and penetrate through everything; so, with greater reason, with the power of the First Author—may his name be exalted. That is why it is said that the First Author is in all beings and that nothing can exist without him.

Part III

Pupil: It seems quite necessary to prove and demonstrate by necessary and universal proofs that the forms that are in the substance that supports the categories are the object of the action of the simple substance and stem from them.

Master: Your request is a good one: it is in fact very necessary. Here are the proofs that demonstrate that the forms borne by the corporeal substance are the object of the action of the simple and spiritual substances and that they stem from them.

The action of every simple substance is simple. Now the actions that are in the substance that supports the categories are simple. Therefore the actions that are in the substance that supports the categories are the object of the action of the simple substance.

The energies, the forms, and the motions that are in the corporeal substance are more simple and more subtle than the corporeal substance. Now all that is more simple and more subtle than the corporeal substance submits to the domain of the simple substance. Therefore the energies, the forms, and the motions that are in the corporeal substance submit to the domain of the simple substance.

Next, I add to this conclusion the following proposition: All that is in the nature of the simple substance must be either of the essence of the simple substance or one of its accidents. Therefore the energies, the forms, and the motions that are in the corporeal substance are either of the essence of the simple substance or of the number of accidents. But they are not of the essence of the simple substance because they are not substances. Therefore they are of the number of its accidents.

The compound substance receives the forms. Now all that receives the forms receives them from the agent that produces them in it. Therefore the compound substance receives the forms of the agent that produces them in it. Then I add to this conclusion this proposition: The simple substance acts upon the compound substance. Therefore the compound substance receives the forms of the simple substance.

When a thing receives something from another thing, the thing received in that which receives is the object of the action of that which gives. Therefore the forms that the compound substance receives are the object of the action of the simple substance. Now everything that in a thing is the object of the action of another thing exists in the causative agent. Therefore the forms that the compound substance receives exist in the causative agent. Now the causative agent is the simple substance. Therefore the forms that the compound substance receives exist in the simple substance.

The forms that are borne by the corporeal substance are actions. Now every action comes from that which acts on the forms that are borne. Therefore the forms that are borne by the corporeal substance do not come from the substance that supports the categories. Similarly I add to this conclusion the following proposition: Everything that does not come from something comes from its contrary. Therefore the form that is borne by the corporeal substance comes from its contrary. Next, I add to this proposition: The simple substance is opposed to the compound substance. Therefore the forms borne by the corporeal substance come from the simple substance.

If the compound substance does not take from the simple substance the motions, energies, and figures, the simple substance either does not exist, or does not act. But the simple substance exists and acts. Therefore the compound substance takes from the simple substance the figures, energies, and motions.

The figures, energies, and motions that are in the compound substance are received necessarily either from the First Author, or from the essence of the substance that possesses them, or from another substance intermediary between them.

If they were received from the essence of the First Author, it would necessarily follow that the First Author and the substance that supports the categories had something in common, for that which is in the essence of the First Author would be united with the essence of the substance. Furthermore, it would be necessary that there should be multiplicity in the essence of the First Author on account of the multiplicity of the figures, energies, and motions. Now both hypotheses are impossible. Therefore the figures, energies, and motions that are in the substance that supports the categories are not received from the essence of the First Author.

If they were received from the essence of the substance that possesses them, it would be necessary that the substance should at the same time cause the form and receive it, and it would be necessary that it should act in so far as it receives or that it should not act in so far as it receives. If it acted in so far as it received, one and the same thing would act and be the object of the action at the same time: which is impossible. If it did not act in so far as it receives, the whole would not receive the form. But it is a substance entirely formed. Therefore it is impossible that it should not act in so far as it is the object of action. If the substance does not act in so far as it is the object of action, and if the agent is stronger than the object of the action, it is necessary, if the substance is one, that the substance be in one way stronger than itself and in another way weaker than itself. If it is not one, and if it acts partly and is partly passive, it is necessary that the passive part should be without form. But the substance in its entirety is formed. It is therefore formed and not formed: which is inadmissible.

In anything composed of two things, each of them can exist by itself. Now the body is composed of substance and form. Therefore the form can exist by itself without the corporeal substance. Similarly I assert: The form can exist by itself without the corporeal substance. Now the form does not exist without a support. Therefore the form is in a support that is not the corporeal substance. Next I add to this proposition: Apart from the corporeal substance, there is no other support except the simple substance. Therefore the form exists in the simple substance.

Every action takes place in the spiritual and every reception in the corporeal. Now if the substance acted in so far as being an object of the action, it would be spiritual and corporeal at the same time. And if it acted partly and was partly the object of the action, it would be partly spiritual and partly corporeal. But the substance that supports the categories in its entirety is corporeal. Therefore there is nothing in it that acts.

If the corporeal substance receives the forms, that are supported in it, from another substance different from itself, it is necessary that this substance should be superior to it. Now the simple substance is superior to the compound substance. Therefore the corporeal substance receives the forms that it has from the simple substance.

The simple substances are perceived only in bodies. Now the forms that are in the compound substance are perceived in bodies. Therefore the forms that are in the compound substance come from the forms of the simple substances.

The form that is perceived by the senses in the compound substance fulfils its being. Now all that fulfils the being of a substance is a substance. Therefore the form that is perceived by the senses in the compound substance is a substance.

The simple substance is divided into matter and form, according to the division of genus into species. Now whenever a thing is divided as the genus is divided into species, the species of this thing receive equally the name and the definition of the genus. Therefore the species of the simple substance receive equally the name and the definition of the genus. To this proposition I add the following one: Matter and form are species of the simple substance. Therefore matter and form receive equally the name and the definition of the simple substance. Now the simple substance receives the name and the definition of the substance. Therefore matter and form receive equally the name and the definition of the substance.

Every effect is composed in relation to its cause. And if the corporeal forms are the effects of spiritual forms, it is necessary that they should be compound. Now they are compound. Therefore they are the effects of spiritual forms.

Whatever was caused is in act in itself, and is in potentiality in the cause. If the forms of the compound substance are effects, it is necessary that they should be in themselves in act and in potentiality in their cause. Now they are effects in act. They are therefore in potentiality in their cause.

The corporeal forms diffused in the substance are united with them. Now a thing, once it is united, has not the same virtue and the same perfection as the simple form by itself. Therefore the form that is diffused in the substance has not a virtue and a perfection so great as the simple form by itself.

Next I take this proposition and I assert: Everything that is not so good as a thing in virtue and perfection is similar to it. Therefore the form diffused in the substance is similar to the simple form by itself.

Then I take this proposition and I add: Everything that is similar to a thing is its reproduction. Therefore the forms diffused in the substance are the reproduction of spiritual forms. Then I add to this proposition: Everything that is the reproduction of a thing is its image or its portrait. Therefore the form that is diffused in the substance is the image or the portrait of the spiritual form.

The forms are simple. Now the simple is anterior to the compound. Therefore the forms are anterior to that which is composed of them.

Every form possessed by matter differs in clarity and in perfection according to the clarity and the perfection of the matter that receives it. Now whenever a thing differs from another thing, the quality of its form depends on the thing from which it differs. Therefore the spiritual form that the matter has depends on the matter from which it differs.

To this proposition I add the following one: Whenever the form of a thing depends on another thing, this form is not a form by itself. Therefore the spiritual form that the matter has is not a form by itself.

Then, after this, I assert: Everything that is not in something by itself is the object of the action of a thing that is in something by itself. Therefore the form that the matter has is the object of the action of a thing that is in another thing a form by itself.

Every spiritual substance has a form and every spiritual substance is subtle. Now the form of every subtle thing emanates from this thing. Therefore the form of the spiritual substance emanates from this substance. Then, after this, I assert: The form of the spiritual substance emanates from this substance. Now whenever the form of a thing emanates from this thing, this form is reflected by the contrary thing that receives it. Therefore the form of the spiritual substance is reflected by the contrary thing that receives it.

To this conclusion I add: Now every form reflected by the contrary thing that receives it penetrates the thing that receives it and envelops it, if its substance is a subtle substance. Therefore the form of the spiritual substance penetrates and envelops the substance with categories. To this proposition I add next: The form of the spiritual substance penetrates and envelops the substance supporting the categories. Now the form borne by the substance supporting the categories penetrates and envelops this substance. Therefore the form borne by the substance supporting the categories is the form itself of the spiritual substance.

Every corporeal substance has a limited essence. Now everything that has a limited essence cannot extend in every place. Therefore the essence of the corporeal substance cannot extend in every place.

Then, inversely: The spiritual substance has an unlimited essence because it is neither quantitative nor finite. Now when a thing has an unlimited essence, the essence extends and exists in every place. Therefore the essence of the spiritual substance extends and exists in every place.

Next, I take this conclusion as a premise and I assert: Now everything that extends, flows and does not remain motionless. Therefore the spiritual substance flows and does not remain motionless. Then I assert: The spiritual substance flows and does not remain motionless. Now whenever a thing flows aril does not remain motionless, the form ceases when it meets a body that obstructs it and that reflects the form and the action of this thing: as the light of the sun, that is reflected by the body. Therefore the form of the spiritual substance ceases and is reflected by the body. Then I add this proposition: The form borne by the corporeal substance ceases in it and is reflected by it. Therefore the form borne by the corporeal substance is the form itself that proceeds from the spiritual substance.

Everything that is reflected from one thing in another has the property of extending on the surface of the thing where it is reflected and of enveloping it to the point of invisibility. Now the form borne by the compound substance extends on the surface of the substance and envelops it to the point of invisibility. Therefore the form borne by the compound substance is the reflection in it of a substance other than it. Then I add to this proposition: Everything that is in a thing the reflection of a thing other than itself exists in that of which it is the reflection. Therefore the form borne by the compound substance exists in the substance of which it is the reflection.

All the designs and the figures that appear in the compound substance are impressed therein by its cause. Now the simple substance is the cause of the compound substance. Therefore all the designs and the figures that appear in the compound substance are impressed therein by the simple substance. Then to this proposition I add the following one: All that is impressed by one thing in another thing exists in the thing that impresses it. Therefore all the designs and the figures that appear in the compound substance exist in that which impresses them. Then I add this proposition: The simple substance impresses the designs and the figures. Therefore all the designs and the figures that appear in the compound substance exist in the simple substance.

The figures, the colors, and the designs that appear in the particular compounds come from an active substance. The substance that has the form of the elements is not active. Therefore the figures, the colors, and the designs that appear in the particular compounds do not come from the substance that has the form of the elements. They come therefore from some simple substance. These actions come from the essence of the simple substance or they do not. If they do not come from its essence, it is possible that they do not come from its action. But it is impossible that they do not come from its action. Therefore it is impossible that they do not come from its essence. And if they come from its essence, it is necessary that they should be in its essence. The same assertion must be made in regard to the universal figures and designs that appear in the compound substance, namely that they exist in the essence of the substance that impresses them.

One is the root of the multiple. The simple substance is one. Therefore the simple substance is the root of the multiple. The forms that are borne by the compound substance are a multitude. Therefore the simple substance is the root of the forms that are borne by the compound substances.

The multiple is an aggregate of units: the units in the aggregate are divided into units as the whole is divided into parts. And whenever a thing is divided into another, the nature of the whole exists in each of its parts. Now the units are parts of the multiple. Therefore the nature of the multiple exists in each of the units.

Now the forms that are borne by the compound substance are a multitude. Therefore the forms that are in the compound substance exist in a single form. But the form of the simple substance is one. Therefore the forms that are in the compound substance exist in the form of the simple substance.

The simple substance resembles unity more than the compound substance does. Now the form that is in the compound substance resembles unity more than the compound substance does. Therefore the simple substance resembles the form that is in the compound substance, since both substances resemble unity more.

Now all similar things are so in genus, species, accident, or quality. But the form is not of the same genus or of the same species as the simple substance, and the simple substance has no accident in its essence. Therefore their similarity does not come from that source. They are therefore similar in relation to the action.

Quantity and quality are two forms. Now every form comes from form. Therefore quantity and quality do not come from the substance that possesses them. Similarly, quantity and quality come from form. Now, apart from the compound substance and the simple substance, there is no form. Therefore quantity and quality come from the simple substance.

Quantity is multitude. Now multitude is composed of units. Therefore quantity is composed of units. Now units are composed of simple unity. Therefore quantity is composed of simple unity. Now simple unity is in the simple substance. Therefore quantity is composed of the unity of the simple substance. The unity in the simple substance is a simple accident. Now the compound accident is composed of the simple accident.

Therefore the compound accident is composed of the unity of the simple substance.

Similarly: Quantity is composed of units. Now compound units are a compound accident. Therefore quantity is a compound accident. To this proposition I add the following one: The compound accident is composed of the unit of the simple substance. Therefore quantity is composed of the unit of the simple substance.

I assert that the properties and the impressions of the simple substance exist in the form that is borne by the compound substance. And here is the proof.

The simple substance is perceived by the senses in the body. Similarly, form is perceived by the senses in the body. A simple substance is one simple being in itself. Similarly, form is a simple unit in itself. The simple substance is a form for the compound substance. Similarly, form is a form for the compound substance. The simple substance completes that of which it is the form. Similarly, the form completes that of which it is the form. The simple substance penetrates the compound substance. Similarly, the form penetrates the compound substance. The simple substance envelops the compound substance.

Similarly with the form. The simple substance distinguishes its subject from another subject. Similarly the form distinguishes the compound substance from another substance. The simple substance gathers together the parts of its subject. Similarly the form gathers together the compound substance. The simple substance is not in place. Similarly with the form. The simple substance is mobile and active. Similarly with the form.

Next, I take this proposition as a premise and I assert that the properties and the impressions of the simple substance exist in the form that is borne by the compound substance. Now wherever the properties of the simple substance exist, this impression is due to the simple substance. Therefore the form that is in the compound substance is impressed by the simple substance.

Similarly, in another way, if the properties and the impressions of the simple substance are in the form that is borne by the compound substance, it is necessary that the form that is borne by the compound substance should impress the properties in the same way as the simple substance does. Similarly, we shall prepare propositions about each property of a simple substance and about the properties of form, and we shall add a proof that concludes that the form comes from the impression of the simple substance. The number of these proofs will depend therefore on the number of the properties from which the propositions arise.

When two substances of contrary form unite, there springs from their union a form different from the proper forms of these substances. The truth of this proposition is evident to the senses: but to the intelligence it will appear in the following manner.

I assert that the forms of two united substances are two. The nature of the two differs from the nature of the one. Therefore the nature of the two forms of the two united substances differs from the nature of each of them. Similarly, in another way, whenever two contrary things unite, they become some kind of one. Now the two differ from the one. Therefore whenever two things unite they become something other than one of them. Next I add to this conclusion the following proposition: Two forms unite. Therefore when two forms unite, they become something other than each of them. Similarly, in another way, the form that springs from the union of two forms must be either one of them or neither the one nor the other. Now it is impossible that it should be one of them because it is impossible that the form should perish. Therefore it is a form that differs from each of them and it is not one of them.

Since the proposition is true that declares that from the union of two substances contrary in form there arises a form that differs from the form of each of them, let us verify the proposition that declares that the simple substance unites with the compound substance. The truth of this proposition is evident to the senses, for we see the impressions of nature and of the soul in the substance that they compose: thus the union and the conjunction of these substances are verified. As for the proof for the intelligence, that is demonstrated in the following manner.

The simple substance is of the same genus as the compound substance. Now everything that is of the same genus unites. Therefore the simple substance and the compound substance unite. Similarly with another method of reasoning. The simple substance acts. Now every agent unites with the thing that receives its action. Therefore every simple substance unites with the thing that receives its action. Then I take this proposition as a premise and I add: Now the compound substance receives the action of the simple substance. Therefore every simple substance unites with the compound substance. Similarly with another method of reasoning. The form of the simple substance emanates necessarily. Now all that emanates necessarily unites with the thing that is before it. Therefore the form of the simple substance unites with the thing that is before it. I take this proposition as a premise and I add the following one: The compound substance is opposite the simple substance. Therefore the form of the simple substance unites with the compound substance. Similarly with another method of reasoning. The simple substance contains the compound substance. Now everything that contains another thing is united with that which it contains. Therefore the simple substance is united with the compound substance. Similarly with another method of reasoning. The simple substance is of unlimited essence. Now whenever a thing is of unlimited essence, its essence is extended. Therefore the essence of the simple substance is extended. And to this conclusion I add: Whenever the essence of a thing is extended, this essence is everywhere. Therefore the essence of the simple substance is everywhere. Now everything whose essence is everywhere is united with everything that the place comprehends. Therefore the essence of the simple substance is united with everything that the place comprehends. Now the compound substance is everything that the place comprehends. Therefore the essence of the simple substance is united with the essence of the compound substance.

Similarly with another method of reasoning. The simple substance wants that which it has in potentiality to pass into act. Whenever a thing wants that which it has in potentiality to pass into act, its effect appears in a subject. Therefore the effect of the simple substance appears in a subject. Now whenever the effect of a thing appears in a subject, this thing unites with this subject. Therefore the simple substance unites with the subject of its action. But the compound substance is the subject of its action. Therefore the simple substance unites with the compound substance.

And since the proposition that asserts that the simple substance and the compound substance are united is certain, I take it as a premise and I add to it this proposition: Whenever two things unite, there springs from their union a form that differs from the form of each of them. This is the proposition that we have previously verified. Therefore from the union of the simple substance and the compound substance there springs a form that differs from the form of each of them. Then I add to this proposition the following one: The figures, energies, and motions that are in the compound substance are forms that differ from the form of the essence of the simple substance and from the form of the essence of the compound substance, as it was previously. Therefore from the union of the simple substance and the compound substance there spring the figures, energies, and motions that are in the compound substance.

The forms that are in the compound substance pass into action and are perceived by the senses. Now whenever a simple substance unites with the compound substance, the forms that the intelligence seized in it pass from potentiality into act and are perceived by the senses. Therefore the forms that are in the compound substance pass into act and are perceived by the senses when the simple substance unites with the compound substance.

Every corporeal substance is sensible. Now all the impressions that are in a sensible thing are sensible. Therefore all the impressions that are in a corporeal substance are sensible.

Similarly: The impressions of the simple substance are in the corporeal substance. Now all the impressions that are in the corporeal substance are sensible. Therefore all the impressions of the simple substance in the compound substance are sensible. Then I convert this proposition and I obtain the following one: All that is sensible in the corporeal substance is the impression of the simple substance.

All the forms that are in the corporeal substance are sensible. Now all that is sensible in the corporeal substance is the impression of the simple substance. Therefore all the forms that are in the compound substance are the impressions of the simple substance.

The compound substance is an effect. Now all the forms that appear in an effect are impressed therein by its cause. Therefore all the forms and the impressions that appear in the compound substance are impressed therein by its cause. The simple substance is the cause of the compound substance. Therefore all the forms and the impressions that appear in the compound substance are impressed therein by the simple substance.

The form of every effect is in the cause of this effect. Now the simple substances are the causes of the compound substances. Therefore the forms of the compound substances are in the simple substances.

The simple substance is the active cause of the compound substance. Now all that is an active cause for a thing impresses in it that which is in its essence. Therefore the simple substance impresses in the compound substance that which is in its essence. Then I take this proposition as a premise and I assert: The simple substance impresses in the compound substance that which is in its essence. Now the simple substance impresses in the compound substance the figures, energies, and motions. Therefore the figures, energies, and motions are in the simple substance.

Motion is an impression of the soul. Now motion is in the compound substance. Therefore the impression of the soul is in the compound substance.

The imperfect is created by the perfect. Now the imperfect compound substance comes from the simple substance. Therefore the compound substance is created by the simple substance.

The soul moves. Now the mobile is the cause of that which is at rest. Therefore the soul is the cause of that which is at rest. The compound substance is at rest. Therefore the soul is the cause of the compound substance. The compound substance and the forms that are borne by it are together. Therefore the soul is the cause at the same time of the compound substance and of the form that subsists in it.

Every corporeal substance is receptive only and compound only, while the spiritual substance is receptive and active, simple in one sense and compound in another sense. Now that which is active and receptive, simple and compound, receives numerous forms. And if a thing receives numerous forms, these numerous forms are in it potentially. There are therefore in the simple substance numerous forms in potentiality. Now all that in which there are numerous forms in potentiality causes these forms to pass from potentiality into act. Therefore the simple substance causes the forms that are in it in potentiality to pass into act.

It is therefore necessary that every cause should impress the figures and its forms in its effect. Now that which receives an impression never equals in force and perfection that which gives it. It is therefore necessary that the cause should be equipped with more figures and forms than its effect. Now the simple substance is the cause of the compound substance. It is therefore necessary that the simple substance should be equipped with more figures and forms than the compound substance. Similarly, in another way, the compound substance is the effect of the simple substance. Now the effect is equipped with fewer figures and forms than its cause. Therefore the compound substance is equipped with fewer figures and forms than the simple substance. Similarly, in another way, if the simple substance had only a single figure and a single form, its effect would be equipped with more forms and more figures. But the effect is not equipped with more forms and figures than the cause. Therefore the simple substance has one figure only and one form only.

Part IV

All that has more than a single figure to contain it can receive all the figures. And whenever a thing receives all the figures, every form is in its essence. Now the simple substance receives all the figures. Therefore every form is in the essence of the simple substance.

All that receives numerous forms has not in itself one form that is peculiar to it. Now the simple substance, like the soul, the intelligence, nature, and matter, receives numerous forms. Therefore none of them has in it a form that is peculiar to it.

The spiritual simple substance is more apt to combine in itself numerous forms than the corporeal compound substance. Now the corporeal substance and the corporeal figure unite numerous forms and figures.

All that is perceived in action in a thing was in potentiality before passing into act. Now the forms that are in the compound substance are in it in act. Therefore they were in potentiality before passing into act.

The universal soul that unites the faculties of the soul is more apt to have numerous forms than one of its faculties. Now the visual faculty among the faculties of the soul has numerous forms. Therefore the universal soul is more apt to have numerous forms than the visual faculty.

If sense is a faculty that embraces the sensible forms, it is necessary that the soul should be a substance that embraces the aggregate of the forms. Now the sensitive faculty embraces the sensible forms. Therefore the substance of the soul embraces the aggregate of the forms.

The more simple and subtle the substance is, the more it embraces forms: thus the soul, the intelligence, and the primal matter. Now the substance of the soul is more simple and more subtle than the compound substance. Therefore the substance of the soul embraces more forms than the compound substance.

Whenever a substance seizes the aggregate of the forms, all the forms are in its essence absolutely. Thus matter, intelligence and soul seize all the forms that are borne by the compound substance. Therefore all the forms are in the essence of the soul.

If the intelligence perceives the spirituality of things, this perception occurs through resemblance. Therefore the intelligence is similar to the power of everything. And if it is similar to the power of everything, the form of everything is in it. Similarly with the soul.

The intelligence and the soul know all things. Now knowledge is the subsistence in the soul and in the intelligence of the form of the thing known. Therefore the forms of all things subsist in the soul and in the intelligence. Now the forms subsist in them by union. Therefore all the forms are united with the intelligence and the soul. Now the union takes place through resemblance. Therefore all the forms are similar to the intelligence and the soul.

The intelligence and the soul conceive knowledge from the forms of things. Now all that conceives something conceives it through its form. Therefore the intelligence and the soul conceive the forms of things by their form, and their knowledge of the forms of things is due to the union of their form with the forms of things. Therefore the intelligence and the soul unite their form with the forms of things. Now all things that unite are similar. Therefore the forms of the intelligence and the soul are similar to the forms of things.

Sensible things are in the soul simply, for their forms are in it without their matter. Similarly the forms of things are in the intelligence more simply and in a more general fashion. Therefore the inferior forms must be in all the superior forms, degree by degree, until the universal form is reached in which exists the aggregate of all the forms. But the superior forms are not in place, while the inferior forms are in place; the first participate in the union of the spiritual substance, while the second participate in the dispersal of the corporeal substance.

The sensitive soul perceives the sensible forms without perception of the matter that is their subject: and this is the case because the matter is outside the essence of the soul and the forms are in the essence of the soul. Hence I shall propose and say: If the soul does not perceive the matter that has the forms because the matter is outside its essence, it is necessary that the object of its perception should be the forms that are in its essence. Now the soul does not perceive the matter because it is outside its essence. Therefore it perceives the forms because they are in its essence.

If the sensible forms were not similar to the soul, the soul would not receive them and these forms would not subsist in it. But the soul receives these forms and they subsist in it. Therefore they are similar to it.

The sensible forms that are in the compound substance are in the soul simply, for the forms are in it divested of their matter. They are similarly in the intelligence, but more absolutely. Now the substance of the soul is superior to the substance that has the sensible forms. It is therefore necessary that the inferior forms should be in the superior substances.

The forms that are in the compound substance are sensible in act for the soul. Now all that is in act was previously in potentiality. Therefore the forms that are in the compound substance in act were previously in potentiality in the substance of the soul. Now all that is in potentiality is spiritual with regard to that which is in act. Therefore the forms that are in potentiality in the substance of the soul are spiritual with regard to the forms that are in act. Now the forms that are borne by the compound substance are in act. Therefore the forms that are in potentiality in the substance of the soul are spiritual with respect to the forms that are borne by the compound substance.

If the substance of the intelligence and that of the soul detach the forms that are borne by the compound substance and carry them in themselves divested of the substance that carries them, it is necessary that these forms should be in the essence of each of them. Now the soul and the intelligence detach the forms that are carried by the compound substance. Therefore these forms are in the essence of each of them.

If the particular form borne by the particular matter subsists in the substance of the particular soul divested of the matter that it bears, it is also necessary that the universal form borne by the universal matter, that is, the form borne by the compound substance, should be borne by the substance of the universal soul divested of the universal matter, that is, of the compound substance that bears it. The same assertion must be made of the forms of the universal soul borne by the substance that is superior to it, until the primal substance is reached that bears all things: for the case of the universal form is the same as the particular form.

If everything has a spiritual matter and a spiritual form, it is necessary that they should exist in everything: and if they exist in everything, it is necessary that there should be in each corporeal substance a spiritual matter and in each corporeal form a spiritual form. It is therefore necessary that in the corporeal color and in the corporeal figure there should be a spiritual color and,a spiritual figure and it is necessary that the spiritual color and the spiritual figure should subsist in the spiritual substance.

The corporeal forms emanate from the spiritual forms. Now all that emanates from something is the image of the thing from which it emanates. Therefore the corporeal forms are the image of the spiritual forms.

All that emanates from some origin is united with the origin and dispersed far from the origin. Now the sensible forms are united with the spiritual substances and dispersed in the corporeal substances. Therefore the sensible forms derive from the spiritual substances and are nearer their origin in the spiritual substances than in the corporeal substances.

The forms dispersed in the corporeal substances are united with the spiritual substances. Now all that is dispersed in something is united with its origin. Therefore the spiritual substances are the origin of the forms that are dispersed in the corporeal substances.

The spiritual substances unite the sensible forms. Now every origin unites that of which it is the origin. Therefore the spiritual substances are the origin of the sensible forms.

All that derives from some origin is united with its origin. Now the sensible forms are united in the spiritual substances. Therefore the sensible forms derive from the spiritual substances.

The sensible forms unite. Now all that derives from an origin unites. Therefore the sensible forms derive from an origin. Now all that derives from an origin unites with the origin. Therefore the sensible forms unite with their origin. Now the sensible forms unite with the spiritual substances. Therefore the spiritual substances are the origin of the sensible forms.

Whenever a thing is an origin for another thing, the latter unites with it essentially. Now the sensible forms unite essentially with the spiritual substances. Therefore the spiritual substances are the origin of the sensible forms.

The sensible forms unite essentially with the spiritual substances. Now all that with which things unite essentially constitutes the origin of these things.

Therefore the spiritual substances are the origin of the sensible forms.

The simple substance, like the soul and the intelligence, perceives the essences of the sensible forms by itself. Now whenever a thing perceives the essence of another thing by itself, the essence of the first thing unites with the essence of the second thing. Therefore the essence of the simple substances unites with the essence of the sensible forms. Then I take this proposition as a premise: The essences of the simple substances and of the sensible forms are united: and whenever two essences are united, they form one. Therefore the essence of the simple substances and the essence of the sensible forms are one. Then I shall propose and say: the essence of the simple substance and of the sensible forms is one. Now whenever a thing emanates from another thing, its essence and that of the thing from which it emanates are one essence. Therefore the sensible forms emanate from the essence of the simple substance.

The union of the forms of things is much greater in the form of the intelligence than in the other forms. Now all that derives from an origin is more united with its origin than different from it. Therefore the form of the intelligence is the origin of the aggregate of the forms.

Every form that springs from the soul in matter was previously in the soul spiritually and it is to these spiritual forms that the corporeal forms owe their existence. Now the soul creates the forms and the corporeal figures that are borne by matter. Therefore these forms and these figures are in the soul spiritually.

The Master proceeds: We have just adduced as far as possible the proofs that demonstrate (A) that the forms borne by the compound substance are impressed therein by the simple substance, which is superior to the compound substance: and they have all established (B) that these forms exist in the essence of the simple substance that impresses them and that they emanate and originate from this substance. We have demonstrated this synthetically. Now we shall also present the analytical proof, resolving the impressions that are in the compound substance and noting for each of them the simple substance whose characteristic is to produce it: for when we have done this, we shall know how many simple substances there are united with the compound substance, that impress in it its designs and figures.

Pupil: By the cumulative proofs that you have just presented, you maintained (B) that the sensible forms that are borne by the compound substance exist in the essence of the simple substance that impresses them: (C) you affirmed also that these forms are united in the essence of the soul and in that of the intelligence and that they emanate from these substances, and you postulated as a proof of this the faculty of the soul and of the intelligence to perceive all these forms. Show me then how it is possible that the sensible forms, like continuous quantity, figure, color, and the first qualities are united in the essence of the simple substance and how the faculty of the simple substance to perceive all these forms is proof that they are united and that they subsist in it, for to me nothing is more inadmissible than to say that the forms of this sensible world, however great and numerous they may be, exist in the substance of the soul and that of the intelligence. Show me this then, to the best of your ability.

Master: Do you consider it certain, after the proofs that we have established, that the sensible forms are impressed by the simple substance?

Pupil: I consider it quite certain.

Master: Since the simple substance impresses these forms, it is necessary that it should impress either that which is in its essence only, or that which is in its essence and in the essence of the compound substance, or that which is not in its essence. But it does not impress that which is not in its essence. If indeed it impressed that which is not in its essence, it would be false to say it impresses, for that which impresses gives to the object impressed what it has in its essence. Or again: If the simple substance impressed that which is not in its essence, its action could not be an impression and this substance would create from nothing. But the First Author, sublime and holy, alone creates from nothing.

Pupil: Then assume that the simple substance impresses that which is in the compound substance.

Master: The essence of the compound substance has no form and that is why it receives the impression of the simple substance. For if it has a form, it receives it or not. Now if it receives it and if it is impossible for it to receive it by itself, it is necessary that it should receive it from something else. And if it does not receive it, the form and the essence of the substance are one thing: the form would be therefore the substance itself and the substance the form itself: which is inadmissible. In short, the substance is subject and receptivity, and before the existence of the form in it, it had only the possibility of receiving it from something else.

And in this way the proposition is also refuted according to which the simple substance impresses that which is in its essence and in the essence of the compound substance. And since the proposition according to which the simple substance impresses that which is not in its essence is negated, just like the proposition according to which the simple substance impresses that which is in its essence and in the essence of the compound substance, the proof compels you to say that the simple substance impresses that which is in its essence only.

Pupil: If the proof compels me to say that the sensible forms exist in the essence of the simple substance, be careful that it does not constrain me to maintain that they are in the essence of the simple substance as they are in the compound substance.

Master: It is impossible that the form of the quantity, that figure, color, and the four qualities should be in the simple substance as they are in the compound substance, for it would follow that the simple substance would be similar in its form to the compound substance. But these forms are in the simple substance in a much more subtle and some simple manner. They are in it in so far as forms separated from their matter, perceived by the soul and divested of their substance. These forms are in fact more subtle and more simple than the forms borne by their matter, since they are borne by the essence of the soul divested of the corporeal matter. And since these simple forms have energies emanating necessarily, as has been proved, when these energies spread on the substance that is opposed to them, and when they unite with it, from their emanation on it and from their union with it arise the sensible forms borne by the compound substance. And the cause of the existence of these sensible forms is their union with the corporeal substance. That is why they differ from the simple forms borne by the simple substance. And just as from the union of the simple bodies with the simple substances a form arises that is different from the different forms, so from the union of the simple substances with the compound substances there arises a form different from the different forms which is similar to the union of the light of the sun with bodies whose substance and colors differ, since from their union come lights that differ from the light of the sun and from each other.

Pupil: How can I imagine that this sensible form, so great and extended, that the corporeal substance has, can exist in the simple substance?

Master: Do not be surprised at this. For if the particular simple substance, that is, the particular soul, comprehends the universal compound substance and all the forms, and if it makes it stay in its essence, all the more so must the universal simple substance, that is, the universal soul, comprehend the compound substance and all its forms. Now I see that all the forms of the compound substance, so great and extended, are like an indivisible point to the form of the simple substance. If then this great form is plunged into the indivisible part of the universal simple substance, that is, into the particular soul, there is no reason for being surprised at its presence in the universal simple substance, that is, in the universal soul. For just as the forms of sensible things are in the substance of the universal soul simply, that is, divested of their matter, so there is no reason to be surprised that these forms are plunged into the universal simple substance superior to this substance, or the substance of the intelligence: for the forms of all things are in the substance of the intelligence in a more universal and more simple manner. The forms that are in a superior substance are more united and do not occupy place. Inversely, those that are in the inferior substance are more dispersed and occupy place: the cause of this is the unity of the essence of the corporeal substance: and this occurs only through the union of the essences of the simple substances and the diffusion of the essence of the corporeal substance. And in general the inferior forms are enveloped by the superior forms, to the point where all the forms are reduced to the universal primal form that unites in it all the forms and in which all the forms are enveloped. Thus the universal form of the intelligence has all the forms and all the forms subsist in it, as I shall show you in what follows, when we examine what the form of the intelligence is and how it perceives all the forms.

Pupil: What you say makes me understand that the sensible forms are in the intelligible forms. But I entertain the following doubt: If all the corporeal forms are in the spiritual forms, more simply than in the corporeal substance, and if the inferior is the image of the superior and is in it, how can the ten corporeal genera be in the spiritual substance?

Master: Consider the inferior extremity of being, that is, each of the genera that are at the inferior extremity and consider likewise its superior extremity: and you will find for every genus of those things that are in the inferior extremity what is contrary to it in the superior extremity. You will find the universal matter corresponding to the substance. You will find the quantity corresponding to the form of the intelligence, as it results from that which precedes. You will find it corresponding also to the units that are borne by the forms of the substance. You will likewise find the seven simple species of quantity corresponding to the number seven of the simple substances, namely, matter, form, intelligence, the soul and nature, and to the number of faculties of each of these substances. You will find the quality corresponding to the differences and to the forms of these substances. You will find the relation corresponding to the fact that they are causes and effects. You will find time corresponding to eternity. You will find space corresponding to the order of these substances that precede and follow each other. You will find location corresponding to subsistence. You will find the action corresponding in these substances to the faculty of impressing, communicating, and creating. You will find the object of the action corresponding in them to the impression from these substances. You will find possession corresponding to the existence of the universal form in the universal matter, to the existence of each of the forms of the simple substance in the matter that possesses it and to the existence, in each of these substances, of the faculties that are peculiar to it. Do you not see that the correlations that I point out to you or the opposition that there is between the forms of the compound substance and the forms of the simple substance prove that the forms of the compound substance emanate from the forms of the simple substance?

Pupil: Yes: that is the proof of what you said. Thanks to you I understand better the existence of the corporeal forms in the simple substance. You have in fact told me that these forms do not become corporeal and do not become so except by uniting with the corporeal substance. For they are similar to a white cloth, thin and transparent, that, applied on a black or reddish body, assumes its color and changes in respect of sensation, but not all in itself.

But show me how the perception that the intelligence and the soul have of the sensible forms constitutes the proof that these forms exist in their essence and that they emanate and come from them.

Master: Did you grant or not that the substance of the soul and of the intelligence is a simple substance and that it perceives all the forms?

Pupil: That is necessarily so.

Master: Does the simple substance that perceives all the forms either perceive them by itself or not perceive them by itself?

Pupil: It must be so.

Master: If one said that the simple substance does not perceive by itself the aggregate of the forms, it would be necessary in consequence that it should not perceive them throughout all time.

Pupil: We assert that the soul does not perceive the sensible things throughout all time and however it may be, but that at times it perceives them and at other times it does not, and that it does not do so in every way.

Master: The soul is not prevented sometimes from perceiving the forms by itself. It would be if it perceived them by anything else but that whereby it does perceive them. The proof of this is that if the soul were prevented sometimes from perceiving the forms by itself, it would be impossible for it to perceive them sometimes by itself. And it would be necessary for it to perceive them by itself and at the same time not to perceive them by itself: which is impossible. Now this is the method of reasoning. It is impossible that at the same time the soul should perceive the forms by itself and should not perceive them by itself. Now the soul perceives the forms by itself. Therefore it is impossible that it should not perceive them by itself. And to this conclusion I add the following proposition: It is said of the soul that it is prevented from perceiving the forms. The conclusion is therefore: The soul is not prevented from perceiving the forms by itself. Therefore it is necessary that it should perceive the forms by itself. It is therefore evident that the soul perceives the forms by itself.

Pupil: If the soul perceives the forms by itself, it is necessary that in it they should always be in act. But the forms in the soul are not always in act. Therefore it does not perceive them by itself.

Master: If the forms in the soul were in act, they would always be sensible. And the perception by itself that the soul has of the forms does not make it necessary that these forms should be in act in it, for it is not impossible that they are there in potentiality and that the soul then perceives them by itself when they pass into act.

Pupil: How is it possible for the forms to be in the essence of the soul in potentiality and then to be in its essence in act?

Master: Why should that not be possible, since it is a matter of two different times?

Pupil: If the forms are in the essence of the soul in potentiality, how is it possible for the soul to act on them and fail to impress them?

Master: The forms that are in the essence of the soul are not those on which it acts: on the contrary, the forms that are in the bodies act on the essence of the soul and this action is possible because these forms differ from the essence of the soul.

Pupil: Then if the forms are in the essence of the soul, why does it not perceive them without an organ, as the intelligence perceives things without an organ?

Master: The forms that are in the essence of the soul are not the forms borne by the bodies, for these forms are corporeal in act, and that is why the soul requires an organ to perceive them. The intelligence too does not perceive all things without an organ, since it requires the organ to perceive the sensible forms.

Pupil: You have forced me to grant that the substance of the soul perceives the forms by itself. But what do you say of the substance of the intelligence?

Master: If the substance of the soul perceives the forms by itself on account of its simplicity and its spirituality, all the more so is it necessary that the substance of the intelligence should perceive the forms by itself, since the substance of the intelligence is of far greater simplicity and spirituality than that of the soul, and that is why it knows all things by itself.

Pupil: All that you have just said makes me understand that the simple substance perceives all the forms by itself. But what follows?

Master: It follows that the forms exist in its essence.

Pupil: What is now the method of reasoning?

Master: The method of reasoning is as follows: The simple substance perceives all the forms by itself. Now whenever a substance perceives things by itself, between it and that which it perceives there is no intermediary. Therefore between the simple substance and the forms that it perceives there is no intermediary. Then I assert: The forms that the simple substance perceives by itself without an intermediary either subsist in its essence or are next to its essence. But it is not possible that they should be next to its essence, for they require a support that bears them and there is no other support except the essence of the substance of the soul. Therefore the forms subsist in the essence of the soul.

This becomes still more evident if it is observed that the simple substance is similar to the forms in this respect that the forms are in themselves simple and spiritual and that they become corporeal only through the corporeal matter that they bear. Now the concept of similar things implies that they join and unite together. It is therefore necessary that the forms should unite with the simple substance. Now if the forms unite with the simple substance, they are then with the essence of this substance a single thing. And if the essence of the forms and the essence of the simple substance are a single thing, it is necessary that the forms should be in the essence of the simple substance.

The following arguments can make this proposition still more evident. All that has an interior and an exterior is a compound substance, and every compound substance has an interior and an exterior. And if we add to one of these propositions the following one; The simple substance is not a compound, it follows; Therefore the simple substance has neither an interior nor an exterior. Therefore there is not something in the interior or in the exterior of its essence. Therefore there is nothing in the interior or the exterior of its essence. And to this conclusion I add this proposition: All the forms are in the simple substance. Therefore the forms that are in the simple substance are not in the interior or in the exterior of its essence. To the preceding conclusion I add this proposition: Whenever a thing is not in the interior or in the exterior of another thing and it is yet in it, the essence of this latter thing and the essence of that which is in it are one essence. Therefore the forms that are in the simple substance and the essence of this substance are one thing.

The following arguments clarify this proposition still more. The simple substance perceives the form through union. Now the union of the substance with the form occurs through motion. Therefore the simple substance perceives the forms through motion. Now all motion is in time. Therefore the simple substance perceives the forms in time. Now all that perceives something in time perceives many dispersed things in more time than a single thing. Therefore the simple substance perceives numerous forms dispersed in more time than it takes to perceive only one form. Now all that perceives numerous forms dispersed in more time than it takes to perceive only one form cannot perceive at the same time numerous forms dispersed. Therefore it is impossible that the simple substance should perceive at the same time numerous forms dispersed.

To this conclusion I add this proposition: The simple substance perceives by itself numerous forms at the same time. Therefore the numerous forms that the simple substance perceives at the same time are not these forms dispersed. To this conclusion I add the following proposition: The sensible forms in the corporeal substances are dispersed. Therefore the forms that the simple substance perceives at the same time are not in the forms that are in the corporeal substances.

Similarly in another way, the numerous forms that the simple substance perceives at the same time are not dispersed. Now the forms that are not dispersed are in the essence of the simple substance. Therefore the numerous forms that the simple substance perceives at the same time are in the essence of the simple substance.

Similarly in another way, the forms that the simple substance perceives at the same time must necessarily be united. Now the united forms are in the simple substance. Therefore it follows necessarily that the forms with which the simple substance unites are in the simple substance.

The same proposition can be clarified still more by the following method of reasoning. The numerous forms that the simple substance perceives unite spiritually with its essence. Now the essence of the simple substance is united spiritually. Therefore the forms that the simple substance perceives are united spiritually. Now all things united spiritually exist in a thing united spiritually. Therefore the numerous forms that the simple substance perceives exist in a single thing, united spiritually. Now the simple substance is a single thing, united spiritually. Therefore the numerous forms that the simple substance perceives exist in the simple substance.

The same proposition is again proved by the following reasoning. The simple substance perceives all the forms by itself. Now the form of everything is the thing itself. Therefore the simple substance perceives all the forms by its form. Then I assert: The simple substance perceives all the forms by its form. Now it perceives all the forms by its form when its form unites with these forms. Therefore the form of the simple substance unites with all the forms. Similarly I assert: the form of the simple substance unites with all the forms. Now whenever the form of a thing unites with all the forms, this form comprehends all the forms with which it is united. Therefore the form of the simple substance comprehends all the forms with which it unites. To this conclusion I add the following proposition: The form of the simple substance comprehends all the forms with which it unites.

Now whenever a thing comprehends many forms, these numerous things that it comprehends exist in it. Therefore all the forms that the simple substance comprehends exist in it. Then I take this conclusion and I assert: All the forms are in the form of the simple substance. Now the form of the simple substance is its essence. Therefore all the forms are in the essence of the simple substance.

The same proposition is clarified again by the following reasoning: The sensible forms are effects of the form of the simple substance. Now every effect is in its cause. Therefore the sensible forms are in the form of the simple substance. Now the form of the simple substance is its essence. Therefore the sensible forms are in the essence of the simple substance.

Pupil: All the arguments that you have just advanced make me understand that the sensible forms are in the essence of the simple substance from the fact that the simple substance perceives all the forms by itself. But another doubt assails me. Did you mean that the simple substance perceives all the forms by itself although these forms are in their support and not in it, and that thus, when the simple substance wants to imagine them by itself and it takes up a position by itself confronting them, it perceives what these forms are although they are not in it?

Master: Is it possible that the essence of the substance perceives the form while the essence of one does not unite with the essence of the other to become a single thing?

Pupil: It can be very well said that the essence of the substance perceives the form although it is different from it: thus, when it perceives the sensible forms divested of their matter, although these forms are very different from it, it imagines them nevertheless necessarily, perceives and represents them to itself as if they were present in it.

Master: When a form is perceived, it signifies that the essence of the substance is impressed by the form. Now the impression results from the conjunction of the impresser and the impressed.

Therefore when a form is perceived by the substance, it is the result of their conjunction and union with each other.

Pupil: If the form unites with the essence of the simple substance, it is necessary that the form that unites should be the form borne by the matter of another form. If this form is that which is borne by the matter, it cannot unite with the essence of the substance except by separation from the matter. But it does not separate from the matter. Therefore it does not unite with the essence of the substance. If on the contrary the form that unites with the essence of the substance is not the form borne by the matter, then it is false to assert that the form borne by the matter is the form that is in the essence of the simple substance.

Master: The union of the form borne by the matter with the essence of the substance is not a corporeal union like its union with the matter, so that the form cannot unite with the essence of the simple substance except by separation from the matter. But this union is a spiritual union. For the form of this form unites with the essence of the form that is in potentiality in the essence of the simple substance, by means of which this form in potentiality passes into act.

Pupil: I understand that it is impossible that the simple substance should perceive the forms without their being in it. But I am worried about the concept of a single thing that assimilates with all things, that is all things, that bears and contains all things without contracting or thickening. And I should like you to show me how many things exist in one simple thing, so that I can grasp this doctrine and increase my enjoyment.

Part V

Master: You will understand how many things exist in one simple thing when we discuss the form of the universal intelligence that bears the aggregate of all the forms. You will then know how the inferior things exist in the superior things and the parts in the whole. And from there you will come to know how all the forms subsist in the universal matter and how the universal matter and the universal form, with all that is contained therein, subsist in the will of the First Author, holy and sublime. Listen therefore now to the proofs that demonstrate the existence of many things in one simple thing.

The numerous forms assembled in the simple substance are simple and spiritual. Now all that is simple and spiritual does not occupy place. Therefore the numerous forms assembled in the simple substance do not occupy place. Then I take this proposition as a premise and I add another one: Whenever a thing does not occupy place, a single one is equal—or several of these things, assembled in the unity that bears them. Therefore a single one is equal—or several of the numerous forms assembled in the simple substance in the unity that assembles and bears them. I take again this proposition as a premise and I add: When a thing is equal—or several of these things, assembled in a single thing, there is no opposition to the union of several of them in a single thing. Therefore there is no opposition to the union in the simple substance of the numerous forms that are assembled therein.

The simple substance and the compound substance are contraries. Now whenever two things are contraries, if something suits one, its contrary suits the other. Therefore if something suits the simple substance, its contrary suits the compound substance. Similarly, I take this proposition and I assert: The compound substance is a corporeal place for the corporeal forms. Now whenever a thing is a corporeal place for another, it is impossible that several things should be there at the same time. Therefore it is impossible that several forms should subsist at the same time in the compound substance. And there is the inverse proof: The simple substance is a spiritual place for the spiritual forms. Now whenever a thing is a spiritual place for another, there is nothing to prevent a multitude of forms from subsisting therein at the same time. Therefore there is nothing to prevent a multitude of forms from subsisting at the same time in the simple substance.

The multiple comes from the one. Now all that comes from something is in that form which it comes. Therefore the multiple is in the one. Similarly, I take this proposition and I assert: The forms of the compound substance are multiple. Now every multiple is in the one. Therefore the multiple forms of the compound substance are in the one. Now the forms of the simple substance are in the form of the simple substance.

The more the substance is simple and one, the more forms it comprehends so that numerous forms are in it: and the more corporeal and multiple the substance is, the fewer forms it receives. From these two principles we shall deduce a single proposition, that asserts: The union of numerous forms does not appear necessarily except with the union of the substance and disappears with it. Then I add this statement:

Whenever a thing does not appear necessarily except with another thing and disappears with it, the second thing is the cause of the existence of the first thing. Therefore the union of the substance is the necessary cause of the assembly in it of numerous forms. Now the union of the simple substance comes from the unity that is in it. Therefore the unity that is in the simple substance is the necessary cause of the assembly in it of numerous forms. Similarly, I take this conclusion as a premise and I assert: Unity assembles numerous forms. Now whenever a thing assembles numerous forms, these numerous forms are in it. There are therefore numerous forms in unity. Then I take this proposition and I assert: There are numerous forms in unity. Now the unity of the simple substance is its form. Therefore numerous forms are in the form of the simple substance.

The form that is more united comprehends more forms. Now the forms of the simple substances are more united than the forms of the compound substances. Therefore the forms of the simple substances comprehend more forms than the forms of the compound substances. Now the forms of the simple substances are one. Therefore the forms that are one comprehend more forms than the forms of the compound substances.

Unity is the sole origin of multiplicity. Now all that is the sole origin of a thing has this thing. Therefore unity has by itself multiplicity. Now whenever a thing has by itself multiplicity, the multiplicity is in it by itself. Therefore multiplicity is by itself in unity. Now the essence of unity is one. Therefore multiplicity is in the essence of the one.

Every form unites what is imagined by it. Now all that unites something does not multiply it. Therefore the form does not multiply that which is imagined by it. And since the form does not multiply, it is necessary that the matter should multiply. Similarly, I take this proposition as a premise and I say: The multiplication of the form is due to the matter. Now there is no matter in the simple substance. Therefore the forms in the simple substance do not multiply themselves. Therefore they unite in it. Similarly, I take this proposition as a premise and I assert: The multiple forms unite in the simple substance. Now nothing prevents all that unites from existing in the single simple substance. Therefore nothing prevents multiple forms from existing in the single simple substance.

The simple substance has no location. Now whenever a thing has no location, its essence is equidistant from everything. And all that is equidistant from everything assumes by itself the forms of all things in one. And whenever a thing grasps by itself the forms of all things at the same time, these forms are in its essence. Therefore the forms of all things are in the essence of the simple substance. Now the forms of all things are numerous. Therefore the numerous forms are in the essence of the simple substance.

The property of continuous quantity is to occupy a place equal to itself. Now whenever the property of a thing is to occupy a location equal to itself, another thing cannot occupy this location so long as the first thing occupies it. Therefore the property of quantity consists in this, that nothing occupies its location so long as it occupies it itself. Now that of which another thing cannot occupy the location, so long as it occupies it, cannot unite with another thing in one location. Therefore the property of quantity is the inability to unite with another thing in one location. Then I take this conclusion as a premise and I add the following proposition: The forms that are in the simple substance are exempt from quantity. Therefore the forms that are in the simple substance unite in one location. The simple substance is not a corporeal location. Now the property of the corporeal location is that numerous things do not unite in it at the same time. Therefore numerous things can unite at the same time in the simple substance.

Forms exist in the spiritual substance in a more noble manner than all their manners of existing in the corporeal substances. Now in the compound substance there is the union of numerous forms in a single subject: as color, figure, line and surface are united in it. Therefore the spiritual substance is more worthy to have in it such a union of forms.

Individuals and species are numerous. Now individuals and species are in the genera. Therefore numerous things are in the genera. Now the genera are a single thing. Therefore numerous things are in a single thing.

If the inferior comes from the superior, the inferior exists in the superior. Now the inferior comes from the superior. Therefore the inferior exists in the superior. Now the inferior is multiple. Therefore the multiple exists in the superior. But the superior is one. Therefore the multiple exists in the one.

The Master continues: We have just adduced the proofs, as far as it was possible, demonstrating that the multiple exists in the one. And it is the proof of which we said: The forms borne by the compound substance exist in the simple substance. Therein also lies the proof of what we wanted to demonstrate, namely, the existence of the simple substances that impress in the compound substance its designs and figures.

Pupil: Although the doubt regarding the union of a multitude of things in a single thing is removed, yet two other doubts have assailed me, that are not smaller than this one. It may be asked how the spiritual forms become corporeal, and how the corporeal accident arises from a spiritual substance.

Master: What we have already said in discussing this question is sufficient. But I am going to repeat it briefly. (1) I assert that whenever two contrary things unite, from their union arises a thing that is not one of them such as they were individually. Now since the simple substance is contrary to the compound substance, it is necessary that from their union there should arise another thing that is not one of them. Such is the form borne by the compound substance, for this form is not spiritual absolutely since it is borne by the corporeal matter. Similarly, it is not corporeal absolutely either, because it is more simple than the matter and can be borne sometimes, divested of matter, by the soul. (2) Furthermore, the corporeal matter is finite and contracted, and whenever a thing is finite and contracted, the form diffused on it by the substance that is before it extends over its surface and exists in it. It is therefore necessary that the form diffused by the simple substance on the corporeal matter should extend on its surface and exist in it, for the form follows the matter by taking on a contour and a figure. Thus, since the matter is in itself corporeal, it is necessary that the form diffused on it by the spiritual substance should also be spiritual. (3) Furthermore, the form regularly penetrates the matter that receives it, when the latter is ready to receive it, because the first form that comprehends all forms penetrates into the first matter and is diffused in it, as has been shown before. For if the matter is subtle, the form is diffused in it, dispersed and hidden, with the result that it escapes the senses. If, on the contrary, the matter is coarse, the form has less power to penetrate it and to be diffused through it. Then the essence of the form contracts and does not divide, so that it becomes sensible on account of its contraction: for when the essence of a thing contracts, this thing becomes corporeal and is presented to the senses: and, inversely, when the essence of a thing divides, it becomes more subtle and evades the senses. (4) The emanation of the spiritual forms on the corporeal forms and the subsequent appearance of the corporeal forms in the corporeal matter may be compared to the emanation of light on bodies and the subsequent appearance of colors.

Pupil: Show me and explain it to me.

Master: It is evident that colors are perceived by their essence and that they are not perceived by their deprivation. Now the cause of this is that light in itself is spiritual and subtle. That is why the essence, that is, its form, is invisible, unless it unites with a body that has a surface, and when it does not unite with a body that has a surface, its form is hidden and evades the senses. Thus the light diffused in the air, whose form is not perceived by the senses before it is diffused over a solid body, for example, the earth, so that the light appears and becomes perceptible. And when the form of the light appears on the surface of the body, the form of the color then appears, borne by it, since it is impossible for the form of the light to appear without the form of the color.

Here is the proof: The form of the light appears when it unites with the surface of the body. And as the surface bears in it the essence of the color, it is necessary that the light that unites with the surface should unite also with the color when it unites with the surface. And it is necessary that the color should appear with the appearance of the light. The argumentation regarding the perception of the light with the color proceeds as follows: The light of the sight unites with the light of the sun on account of its resemblance to it. Now the light of the sun unites with its color. Therefore the light of the sight unites with the color. Similarly with another mode of reasoning. The light unites with the color borne by the surface of the body. Now the light appears when it unites with the surface. Therefore the color appears when the light unites with the surface.

And with God's assistance, consider, following this reasoning, the way in which the spiritual form spreads over the corporeal matter. Compare the spiritual form that is in the simple substance to the light of the sun; compare the form diffused over the matter to the light that is on the surface of the body, and compare the color to the corporeal form that is in the corporeal matter in potentiality, for the color is in the body in potentiality. And by comparing these forms with each other, you will see that the corporeal form that is in the matter in potentiality becomes perceptible when it unites with it in the form emanating from the spiritual form on the matter. Thus the color that is in the body is in potentiality, but becomes perceptible when it unites with it the light emanating from the light of the sun on the body. And you will thus realize that the form emanating from the spiritual form on the matter appears to the sense when it unites with the corporeal form that is in the matter in potentiality, for these two forms become one only, as the light diffused on the surface of the body appears to the senses when it unites with the surface of the body, this light and the color becoming a single thing.

Pupil: Thanks to the four methods that you have enumerated, I understand how the spiritual form becomes corporeal when it unites with the corporeal matter. Show me then how it is possible for an accidental form to come from a spiritual substance.

Master: There are two possible answers to this question. One consists in saying that the corporeal form is not by itself an accident but a substance, since it completes the essence of the matter that bears it, and it is not called accident except by comparison to the matter that bears it.

The second answer consists in saying, admitting that it is an accident, that this form does not emanate from the essence of the simple substance, that is, from the matter that bears the form of this substance, but that it is drawn from its form, which is an accident of the matter that bears it, although it is a substance since it completes the essence of the simple substance. And if it is said of the form borne by the compound substance that it is a substance, it is because it emanates from the form of the simple substance, which is a substance.

Therefore since the form borne by the matter of the simple substance is a substance in itself and an accident because it is borne by the matter of the simple substance, nothing prevents the form emanating from it into the compound substance from also being a substance in itself and also an accident because it is borne by the matter of the compound substance.

Pupil: Why is the primal form called substantial and not substance, when it completes the essence of the matter, which is a substance?

Master: Because it can exist only in the matter in which it subsists.

Pupil: If then the form that subsists in the compound matter is a substance, there is no accident.

Master: It cannot be declared absolutely that the form such as quantity and certain kinds of quality is an accident, for quantity is an inseparable form of the essence of the substance and it completes it, and similarly certain qualities are substantial differences, on which depends the existence of the essence of the substance in which they are. But in respect of the other categories, it cannot be said that they are substances.

Pupil: You have shown me that the forms borne by the compound substance emanate from the simple substance, and you have dissipated the doubts that I had on that score. But what will you say if I return to the charge and declare that the simple substance, like the soul, has no form in itself? If you confront me with the forms set in the essence of the soul, I shall say that these forms are accidents that pass over the essence of the soul, as the forms of light pass through the air, that they are not established in its substance, and that they do not change its essence. On the contrary, these forms touch the soul only on coming from the compound matter. When the latter confronts the soul, it unites its designs with the soul and impresses in it its figures on account of the subtlety of the substance of the soul in itself, and these forms pass through it as the forms reflected by polished bodies reflect them. And since these forms are not essential to these bodies and are only accidents that arise in them, the possibility is hence eliminated of the sensible forms being drawn from the spiritual substances.

Master: Explain this objection and develop it while waiting for the answer to follow.

Pupil: (1) Since all knowledge and all reasoning are founded on simple ideas, that are the ten genera, it follows that all that is imagined by the soul and every utterance depending on these representations must be composed of these simple ideas, according to the various modes of their union and their divers compositions of differences, properties, and accidents. And as the knowledge of these simple ideas consists in the existence in the soul of the forms of each of them, for the soul is a subject for it as the matter is a subject for its forms, it follows that the knowledge must be the generation and the substance of all these forms in the soul, then their union and their division by the differences, properties, and accidents. These forms are therefore similar to the accidents that pass through the substance and succeed each other in it. And since this is the case, since the simple ideas of the union from which the sciences spring and speech arises come from the natural matter and from its accidents, that is, from the substance that supports the categories, (2) the rank of the soul being superior to that of matter, and science signifying the presence in the senses of the sensible forms or the accidents that are in the substance, then the passing of these forms in the imaginative faculty, and finally their impression and their perception in the soul because they have become more subtle and more refined by their double stay in the senses and in the imagination—it follows evidently that the soul has no proper knowledge in itself nor essential forms, but that it receives the forms when they reach it on account of its fineness, simplicity, and subtlety of its substance. And it acquires knowledge only if it is above the matter and its accidents and if its essence unites with the forms of the accidents. And the figures and the designs of the accidents are inscribed first of all in it because they are present and touch it, and they mark in it the impression by which the soul receives the truth of the forms impressed in it through the action of the sensible forms on the senses and through the perception that it has of these forms when they act on it. Thus the sensible forms pass through the soul and do not remain there attached to its being when they act on it (3) and as all the accidental forms are divided in themselves since they are compound and not simple absolutely, they divide and separate also in the essence of the soul and each one is constituted separately. And it is fitting that the constitution of these forms in the essence of the soul should be called ideas since they are made intelligible therein and exist in it. (4) And as the soul is intermediary between the substance of the intelligence and the senses, that the perception of that which is in the intelligence should escape it. Similarly, when it turns toward the intelligence, the perception of that which is in the senses is taken from it, for each of the extremes is opposed to the other, and when the soul approaches one, it recedes from the other, while the forms pass through its essence and succeed each other in its essence, since they are not essential to it, just as the sensible forms pass through the sense of sight, for this sense, turning from some forms toward the others, loses them, and they have no existence in it. Such is my opinion of the forms that exist in the soul. A long explanation would be necessary to establish that these forms on the contrary are essential to the soul and inseparable from its substance. Begin then, now, with the second principle that you postulated before, namely, that the sensible forms exist in the essence of the simple substance.

Master: If you wanted, in your discussion, to exclude from the substance of the soul the intelligible knowledge, that is, the perception by the soul itself of the intelligible forms, the proofs demonstrating that the soul knows by itself prevent you from so doing. I shall briefly recapitulate the principles of these proofs as follows: If the substance of the soul receives the figures and the forms of things, they are in it in potentiality. And if they are in it in potentiality, it knows them by itself. Similarly: If the soul perceives in it the forms without an organ, they are in it in potentiality. Similarly: If men have in common the perception of everything, knowledge is in their essence. Similarly: If men conceive knowledge without being taught, knowledge is in their essence. Similarly: If the soul foresees things before they exist, it knows them by itself. Similarly: If the soul perceives and feels from the beginning of the growth of the body, it then knows by itself. And so with the other proofs that have the same purpose.

If on the other hand you wanted to exclude from the substance of the soul sensible knowledge, that is, the perception of the sensible forms without an organ, that can be done in a certain way. For we did not mean that the sensible forms exist in the substance of the soul without uniting with it by means of the organs established to receive them. The soul can easily perceive these forms without an organ through the imagination, but this happens after it has perceived them by means of the organs.

But we did not intend to imply either that these forms exist in the soul, after they have approached the soul and the soul encloses them, as they subsist in their supports. We mean that the sensible forms are in the soul in potentiality and that these forms are similar to the sensible forms in act and for this reason join and unite with them. And the idea that we express that the sensible form is in potentiality in the substance of the soul explains that the substance of the soul receives the sensible forms and that these forms are impressed in it and unite with it. But when we say that all the sensible forms are in the substance of the soul in potentiality, we do not understand that each of these forms is in it separately, as they are in their corporeal supports: but we mean that the form of the sensible soul is a single simple form that gathers into it all the sensible forms, for this form has the power to bear all the sensible forms in act when they unite with it, and these forms are in it in potentiality. We must not therefore deny that a multitude of forms unite in one single form: we have already given the proofs of this. And what we say about the form of this soul is similar to that which is said of the form of the rational soul and of that of the intelligence: the form of each of these substances unites all the intelligible forms, except that the form of the intelligence unites them more than the form of the soul. And we do not mean that each of these forms is in these substances separately, nor that these forms come to them exteriorly: but we mean that the form of each of these substances is in itself a universal form, or that by nature and essence it perceives and bears every form. And we could not say that all forms exist in the form that unites them, whatever be the form assumed among the forms of the universal substances, if these forms did not exist therein in potentiality.

Pupil: Explain this in still greater detail.

Master: If the simple substance perceives many forms, it perceives them by its form, for if the form of the simple substance perceives many forms, it perceives them either by that which is in it, or by that which is not in it. If it perceives them by that which is in it, then the many forms are in it. If on the other hand it perceives them by that which is not in it, it is possible that a substance other than that of the soul perceives these forms: which is false. Furthermore, if the form of the simple substance perceives the forms by that which is not in it, it is quite unthinkable that this form and the forms that it perceives are in agreement. But if they are not in agreement, they do not unite in any way. Now the concept of agreement of two forms implies that the form of the simple substance is capable of receiving the form that unites with it and that it is prepared to unite with it.

Pupil: All the arguments that you have produced will be valid only when you have established that the soul has a form in itself. But what answer will you give me if I say that the soul has not any form in itself?

Master: Either the simple substance has a form that is peculiar to it, or it has not. Now it is impossible that it should not have a form peculiar to it for it would not exist. In fact, the existence of a thing is always due to the form. Furthermore, if the simple substance had no form peculiar to it, it would not be a species different from the others. For every difference comes from the form. Furthermore, it would not perceive any form, for it is by its form that it perceives the forms.

Now if the simple substance has a special form, either it receives all the forms, or does not receive any, or receives a single form. If it received a single form in act, there would be no difference between the form of the simple substance and that of the compound substance, for the compound substance receives one form only, while the simple substance receives a large number. And if it did not receive any form, the simple substance would not perceive anything. But the evidence shows the contrary. It remains therefore that the simple substance perceives all the forms. Similarly: Since the simple substance has a form, either it differs from every form or it is similar to every form. If it differs from every form, it does not receive any form. But if it is similar to every form: and if it receives every form, all the forms are in it.

Pupil: Why does the substance of the soul not resemble the substance with categories, that I envisage as divested of all forms?

Master: It is not really but ideally that the substance of the categories is divested of form. On the other hand, we do not say of the substance of the soul that ideally it is not divested of form, but we assert that in act or existence it is not, for it is possible to distinguish ideally between the matter and the form of the same, while it is impossible to do so effectively and in existence.

Furthermore, if it is said that the substance of the soul has no form, if it is denied that all forms are in it, and if it is asserted that the forms pass through it as the forms pass through a mirror, it still remains true despite that, that there is a resemblance between the form of the soul and the forms that pass through it. But what would be said of the course of the production of the organs of the soul, and how could the soul be informed if the forms did not dwell in it? What could one say also of the form of intelligence, in which are all the forms by themselves, since no one can say that the knowledge of things is not essential to the intelligence? For the substance of the intelligence is never without knowledge of things. And since it must be granted that the form of the intelligence gathers every form and that all the forms are in it in a more simple way than they are in themselves, why still deny that the form of the soul unites every form? Except that in this respect its rank is inferior to that of the intelligence, for the form of the intelligence is more perfect and more luminous than the form of the soul, although the forms are in the substance of the soul in a more subtle way than in the substance that has the sensible forms.

If we say that all the sensible forms exist in the form of the soul, we must then understand by that, that all the forms are united in its form because the form of the soul by its nature and its being is an essence that unites essentially the essence of every form, for all the forms are united in the concept of the form—all in fact are forms and that is why they are one in the concept of the form— and the concept of the forms is united with the form of the soul, since both are forms: and the particular forms, or the aggregate of the sensible forms, are united with the universal form or the form that comprehends all the forms and the universal form is united with the form of the soul. Therefore the forms that the universal form unites exist in the form of the soul.

Pupil: I see that you have not left me a loophole to deny that all the forms exist in the soul. But what will your answer be to the objection that I raised (2): the knowledge that is in the substance of the soul, I said, proceeds from the accidents borne by the compound substance, and these accidents are not essentially in the soul since the substance of the soul is of a higher rank than the compound substance?

Master: The fact that the substance of the soul is of a higher rank than the compound substance does not prevent the forms from existing in the substance of the soul as well as in the compound substance. But it follows rather that these forms in the compound are dispersed, divided, and not united, and that in the substance of the soul they are joined, not divided, but united. And their union is much greater in the substance of the intelligence, as I shall show you when I discuss the universal form of the intelligence. For these forms in the substance of the soul are intermediary between the corporeal forms borne by the compound substance and the spiritual forms that are in the substance of the intelligence. And the proof of this is that the substance of the intelligence perceives being in all beings, that is, the unifying simple form, or the genera and the species, while the substance of the soul perceives the non-being, that is, the differences, the properties, and the accidents that the senses attain. That is why, when the soul wants to know the being of the thing, it joins and unites with the intelligence in order to acquire through it simple being. And when the soul unites with and attaches itself to the intelligence, their forms unite equally with each other and become a single thing. And as the genus exists in the form of the intelligence, for the genus is the being, and as the difference exists in the form of the soul, for the difference is other than being, and because the one is superimposed on the other or the genus that exists in the intelligence is superimposed on the difference that exists in the essence of the soul, the soul then perceives the being of the thing since the elements of the being, that is, the genus and the difference, unite with its essence: thus it completes the knowledge of the being or of the definition of the thing.

Pupil: Show me how the nine categories, that are the totality of the sensible forms, exist in the substance of the soul and in that of the intelligence.

Master: The nine sensible categories that are in the compound substance exist in it corporeally, dispersed and divided as the senses perceive them in the compound substance. They exist in a more simple manner in the substances of the soul, for they are abstracted from the substance that possesses them: and they still exist in the substance of the intelligence in a more simple manner, for each of them is individually defined by it. Therefore the intelligible form is opposed to the form that exists in the compound substance, since the former is purely substantial and the latter purely corporeal. But the corporeal form is not alien to the concept of the spiritual form, for the spiritual form penetrates the corporeal form interiorly. And the form of the soul is intermediary between these two forms and participates in both extremes. It is spiritual because it is not borne by the compound substance, and corporeal because it is similar in itself to the form borne by the compound substance. And as it is necessary that the forms borne by the compound substance should be in the essence of the soul in a spiritual sense, it is likewise necessary that these forms should be in the essence of the intelligence in a much more spiritual manner. It is also necessary that all the forms, both spiritual and corporeal, should be in the source and origin of the form, that is, in the Will. For every being is in the essence of Perfection and Plenitude: and each substance is a matter and a subject to that which is superior to it and an agent for that which is inferior to it. Just as the corporeal matter is a potency that receives from the soul the sensible forms, so the soul is a receptive power, a matter and a subject in relation to the intelligible form, and the whole is assigned to receive the form of the Will.

As for your idea (4) that the soul perceives that which is in the intelligence when it turns toward it, and perceives that which is in the corporeal matter when it inclines toward this, it is correct. For when the soul inclines toward the corporeal matter, it perceives corporeally and in act the forms that the matter bears, while it perceives them in itself spiritually and in potentiality. And it rises toward the intelligence, it seizes them with intelligent perception, that is, by the knowledge of their definition and what they are. But it does not follow that the passing of the forms in the soul is like the passing of light in the air, so that they are not essential to it, as you thought. For if the forms were not essential to the soul, they would not unite with it and would not pass into act. And here is a proof of the truth of what I say about these forms: The substance of the soul, in dreams, receives from the substance of the intelligence the intelligible forms as the soul does, that is, through the imagination, and in the waking state it perceives them corporeally and materially. And we shall consider in this fashion the being of every inferior in the superior, until the primal matter is reached that possesses everything. But you will learn this when I discuss the universal primal matter and the universal primal form.

Pupil: I know now that the sensible forms exist necessarily in the simple substance and all the doubts that I had on this question are gone. I no longer wonder how the sensible forms are in the substance of the soul, or how these forms must exist in it by virtue of the perception that it has of it, or how a multitude of things is in a single thing. Gone too is the idea that the sensible and intelligible forms that pass into the soul exist in it as the light that passes through the air. And your first proposition is established: The sensible forms that are in the compound substance are impressed by the simple substances. And I know this by the synthetic method. But you promised to show me the same proposition by the analytical method, that is, by resolving the impressions marked by the different simple substances in the compound substance and marked by the simple substances on each other, in order to acquaint me with the quantity and the quality of the simple substances. Begin then this demonstration.

Part VI

Master: I shall now demonstrate the existence of the simple substances according to the impression of the substances upon each other by the analytical method, although by the synthetic method it is quite evident. I ask you first for the two principles that you require in order to understand this.

Pupil: What are they?

Master: Do you grant that the body in itself is at rest and inactive?

Pupil: I would not say otherwise if I did not see simple bodies, such as fire, air, and water, each of which moves in place.

Master: Since the motion of each of them does not come from the fact that they are bodies, but from the fact that they are qualities by the qualities with which they are endowed, you must know that their motions do not in any way prevent the body from being in itself at rest and inactive.

Pupil: What proof is there that the motions of the elements do not come from the fact that the elements are bodies?

Master: If the motions of the elements came from the fact that the elements are bodies, they would not be different.

Pupil: Why so?

Master: If they came from the essence of the body, their motion would be one because the body is one.

Pupil: Why does not the body, which is one, move with different motions?

Master: Because the different motions come from different essences.

Pupil: Why?

Master: Because a single motion depends on a single essence and must not be separated from it except by its destruction. Similarly, a second motion must not come without the first motion being moved aside.

Pupil: Your words make me realize that the motions of the elements do not come from the fact that the elements are bodies, and to me it is an established fact that the body in itself is at rest and inactive. That is one of the principles you ask for. But what is the other?

Master: I ask again whether the action assumes an agent or not?

Pupil: Since the action is an accident that does not exist by itself, it is necessary to say that it has an agent to make it subsist and be.

Master: It is then necessary to grant that the actions that are in the body have an agent other than the body.

Pupil: It cannot be otherwise.

Master: The body is a continuous compound of parts. It is therefore necessary to assert that it has an agent that continues and composes its parts.

Pupil: That is so.

Master: Composition and cohesion come from the motion of the parts of the compound and from their mutual attraction, and also from the fact that each of them is kept in the place where the motion and the attraction have brought it.

Pupil: That is the case.

Master: It is therefore necessary that there should be an essence other than the body, whose property is solely to attract and keep the parts of the body.

Pupil: That is necessary. But show me, by clear proof, that the body is composed of parts.

Master: We learn that the body is composed of parts from the fact that it resolves itself in them ideally, that it divides in seven directions, that it divides in substance, measure and figure and that it has depth in the direction contrary to its natural motion.

Pupil: Add an explanation although this is sufficient.

Master: Between the body dispersed and subtle, and the body contracted and dense there is almost the same relation as between the substance of the intelligence and the sensible substance: and the density of the body comes from the union and the contraction of numerous parts. There is the proof that your question asked for.

Pupil: I understand and I see that there is a substance that composes and unites the parts of the simple body.

Master: What follows then?

Pupil: It follows that this substance composes and keeps the parts of the different bodies, as the elements are composed and kept in minerals, vegetables, and animals.

Master: Observe vegetables and animals again and you will find in them a stronger and more evident action of this substance.

Pupil: Show me this in greater detail.

Master: Do you not see that each of the vegetables and animals requires a matter to supply it with the equivalent of that which it has lost? Hence it requires a faculty to attract the parts of this matter and unite them to the parts of the body. Furthermore, it requires a faculty to retain the parts when they unite with the body. Similarly, it requires a faculty to convert the parts of the matter and assimilate them to the parts in which they assemble. Finally, it requires a faculty to drive out the superfluous matter. It is therefore necessary that there should be in vegetables and animals a substance that effects these operations by means of these faculties.

Pupil: Yes. But what necessity forces me to say that these operations proceed from a single substance and not from different substances, from several faculties and not from one?

Master: If these operations proceeded from many substances, it would be impossible that one of these substances should be higher and more perfect than another, since its operations would not be so. Understand therefore from this that the substance that effectuates is one. Moreover, these operations are of the same genus, for the operation of attraction is of the same genus as the expulsive and digestive operations. As for retention, it is suspension of motion.

Pupil: It is established that these operations come from a single substance. But show me that they come from different faculties.

Master: If this substance had one faculty only, it would have one operation only.

Pupil: Why so?

Master: Because the existence of the action depends on the existence of the faculty: furthermore, because there is a connection of succession between these operations.

Pupil: Now I know that there is one single substance to compose the parts of vegetables and animals and that the operations that appeared in them come from the faculties by which this substance accomplishes its natural operations. But what would you reply to one who said these operations come from the four elements?

Master: We have already said that the body in itself is at rest and inactive.

Pupil: It is the same with the bodies of the elements. But is it then the same with the qualities?

Master: Since the qualities require a mover, understand then that they do not act by themselves.

Pupil: Now I know that there is a substance that composes and retains the parts of the simple body and the compound body and it is established that the substance that acts in two bodies is one, since these two operations belong to a single genus. It is also established that the faculties of this substance differ on account of the diversity of the operations.

Master: Your understanding has been correct. But what follows then?

Pupil: It follows that there exists a universal substance that composes and retains the parts of the universal body.

Master: Whence the necessity?

Pupil: From the necessity by virtue of which the universal body must be similar to the particular single body and to the particular body composed of the elements, on the basis of composition and cohesion. It is therefore necessary to conceive their agent as one.

Master: That is good. But still what follows that statement?

Pupil: The consequence of this is that the universal substance acting on the universal body assigns its essence and its virtue to the particular substance acting on the particular body. Therefore the particular substance corresponds to the universal substance and the particular operation corresponds to the universal operation.

Master: Thus when we see in the particular bodies the presence of some particular action due to a particular substance, will it not be necessary, according to our previous observation, to find also in the universal body the presence of a universal action due to a universal substance?

Pupil: It seems to me that you are referring to the universal substances that you previously called the three souls and the intelligence, substances designated by the particular substances that are in vegetables and animals.

Master: That is just what I wanted to do. But is this a necessary thing or not?

Pupil: When I observe that the particular body requires the universal body and that the particular nature similarly requires the universal nature, since it receives from it being and existence, I see in this respect the particular souls must require the universal souls and the universal intelligence, because they receive from it their being and their existence.

Master: You will find something else by observing that among these substances a higher substance gives to a lower substance.

Pupil: How is that?

Master: The inferior substances envelop the light coming from the higher substance, and the whole envelops the light of the First Author, sublime and holy, as we have already shown when we spoke of the emanation of the substance from others.

Pupil: Acquaint me with the impression of the superior substances on the inferior substances and show me the designs and the figures that they receive from others, by the analytical method, as you promised.

Master: Do you not see in vegetables the motion of growth, of nutrition, and of generation, in which you find the evidence of the substance that causes these motions, that is, the vegetative soul, as the composition and the cohesion of the parts of the body have given you the evidence of the substance that is in the cause, that is, nature?

Pupil: It is clearly so.

Master: Consider likewise the motion of variation in the sense of the motion of thought, that of knowledge and that of reasoning, and you will find therein the evidence of the substances that cause these motions, that is, the animal soul, the rational and intellective soul.

Pupil: By virtue of which is not the substance that causes these actions one, and why do the substances that are in man differ from each other?

Master: Because these substances are separate from each other, for if they were a single substance, vegetables would not be constituted separately with growth, animals with sensation and mobility and men with thought and understanding.

Pupil: Now I know by the procedure that you have just mentioned that these substances differ from each other. But show me how they give to each other and how the operations of these substances belong to the same genus and are similar to each other.

Master: The knowledge of the impression of these substances on each other has two aspects: one is the knowledge of the action and the passivity and the other is the knowledge of the cause of the action and of the passivity. Which one do you want to investigate?

Pupil: Since my intention for the moment is to understand the existence of these substances and to know how they must come from each other, I require at this time only the knowledge of the passivity. I see that the doctrine of the cause of passivity is higher and more noble than the present discussion.

Master: Yes, that is so. Prepare then to understand what you ask, with the aid of the following postulates.

Pupil: I am ready. But what are these postulates?

Master: One of the postulates will teach you that if two things are similar in one relationship and unite in it, although the concept that is common to them is otherwise in one than in the other, it is necessary nevertheless that this concept should be one. Let us consider for example the heat that is in fire and in the part of the air that is near fire. Must the heat that is in the fire be that which is in the air, although differently?

Pupil: It cannot be otherwise.

Master: Then it is not absurd to say that the heat that is in the air comes from the heat that is in the fire, but we must say that it is impressed by it.

Pupil: It is just as you say.

Master: If you realize that substances and their operations differ in a particular way and agree in another way, you must know that the idea in which they agree is one.

Pupil: That is so.

Master: If one of these operations is more perfect than another, must not the more perfect one be the cause of the other?

Pupil: It must be so.

Master: If then you realize that the natural operations belong to the same genus as the operations of the vegetative soul and are similar to them, and that the natural operations are inferior to those of the vegetative soul, must you not grant that the vegetative soul is the cause of nature?

Pupil: It must be so, not only for the vegetative soul and nature, but also for all substances.

Master: Listen then now. I am going to tell you how the operations of these substances belong to the same genus and are similar to each other, so that you will thus understand that they arise from each other.

Pupil: I am listening. I am quite impatient, for I have not met with this doctrine in any philosopher and I think that nothing is more useful and more effective if one wants to attain perfect knowledge of the question that confronts us.

Master: How do you know this?

Pupil: If I find that the actions of these substances belong to the same genus and are similar to each other and that as I pass I rise from the inferior to the superior, thanks to the similarity that exists among the substances, I am presented with the possibility of proceeding to the superior extremity of being and I then discover the principle of motion.

Master: That is true. And you know also the cause of which we have spoken, or the cause of the action and the passivity: you then observe the degrees of the operations: you see that all things obey the divine command and that the good moves all of them.

Pupil: Dear professor, finish then the proof that you promised me of this profound problem, and may the Dispenser of the Good grant it to you.

Master: What is the action whose origin is attributed to nature?

Pupil: The action of attraction and retention, transformation and expulsion.

Master: What is the action that proceeds from the vegetative soul?

Pupil: The action of growth and generation.

Master: What is growth and what is generation?

Pupil: Generation is procreation from the self of a thing similar to itself. Growth is motion of the vegetative parts from the centre toward the extremities.

Master: Now attraction and repulsion are motion in place of the parts of the nutriment by an opposite motion. These actions must therefore belong to the same genus as the motion of the vegetative parts from the centre toward the extremities.

Pupil: That must be so.

Master: Alteration or nourishing is the change of the body of the nourishment from its form and its assimilation to the form of that which is nourished. It is therefore also necessary that this action should belong to the same genus as generation.

Pupil: That must also be so.

Master: Since this is so, it is necessary that one of the substances that produce these actions should impress on the other, one of its faculties, by which it produces its particular effect.

Pupil: It must necessarily be so.

Master: Now what is more perfect acts on the less perfect and marks it with its impression.

Pupil: Yes.

Master: The action of nature is less perfect than that of the vegetative soul.

Pupil: What proof is there?

Master: The proof is that the vegetative soul moves the body in all its extremities, and nature does not do this. Further, the only object of the action of nature is not so perfect as the object of the action of the vegetative soul.

Pupil: You have given me to understand that these actions belong to the same genus. But what do you understand by the retentive faculty in the vegetative soul?

Master: Retention is the resting and weakening of motion.

Pupil: What is the proof of this?

Master: The proof is that motion is stronger than rest. Wherever therefore there is motion, there is power, and where there is rest, there is weakening.

Pupil: What do we gain by this reasoning?

Master: We gain by this, that we understand that the vegetative soul acts on nature because it is more perfect and stronger than it.

Pupil: You have shown me the action of the vegetative soul on nature, and I understand how the actions of these substances belong to the same genus. Show me also the action of the sensitive soul on the vegetative soul and explain how the actions of these substances belong to the same genus.

Master: What is the action of the sensitive soul on the vegetative soul?

Pupil: The action of moving the vegetative parts toward the extremities.

Master: What is the action of the sensitive soul in the animal?

Pupil: Sensation and locomotion.

Master: Is it not necessary that these two motions should belong to the same genus, since the characteristic of each of them is to move the body in place?

Pupil: It is.

Master: Since the action of the animal soul consists in moving the body in its entirety and in making it pass in its entirety from one place to another, and since the action of the vegetative soul consists in moving the parts of the body without displacement of the whole from one place to another is it not necessary that the action of the animal soul should be stronger than that of the vegetative soul?

Pupil: It must be so.

Master: Moreover, the animal soul surpasses the vegetative soul in this respect, that it is united with the forms of bodies that agree with it in subtlety, whether more common or more eminent and draws them out of their corporeal forms, while the vegetative soul unites with the essence of the bodies, because it agrees with them in density and it does so at close quarters only and without an intermediary.

Pupil: That is so.

Master: It is therefore necessary that the animal soul should act on the vegetative soul since it is more perfect and stronger than it.

Pupil: It must be so.

Master: Using the method that I showed you for these three substances, we must similarly discuss the rational soul and the intelligence. And in order not to protract this dialogue, but to bring it into public notice, I shall here condense my talk.

Pupil: Condense it then and give me a general conspectus of it, as you usually do.

Master: The action of the animal soul consists in perceiving the forms of the dense bodies in time, in moving in place, in uttering its voice and in regulating it without the order that indicates understanding. The action of the rational soul is to perceive the subtle forms of the intelligibles, to move in the intelligibles beyond time and space, and to utter its voice, and regulate it in proper order and in a sequence that indicates understanding. Finally, the action of the intelligence is the perception of all the intelligible forms beyond time and space, without inquiry, without effort and without any other reason except its essence, for it is completely perfect.

Pupil: What proof is there that the substance of the intelligence differs from the rational soul?

Master: You must first examine that which proves that the intelligence is a substance. But that is not relevant to the purpose of our investigation. As for the proof that the substance of the intelligence differs from the substance of the rational soul, it is the very proof by virtue of which the rational soul differs from the animal soul and from the vegetative soul. Furthermore, the proof of this is that the rational soul perceives the exterior while the intelligence perceives the essence. Now the essence is more simple than the exterior. Therefore the form of the intelligence is more simple than the form of the soul.

You see then, if you have understood, the action of the intelligence on the rational soul and the action of the rational soul on the animal soul, and you know how the actions of these substances belong to the same genus and are similar.

Pupil: I think you have made me understand. But I am going to show you what I mean.

Master: Say then what it is.

Pupil: I find that the substance of the intelligence is the most subtle and the most perfect of the intelligible substances: that it possesses every form: that it unites with everything, that it perceives and knows everything. I find that the rational soul is inferior to it in that it has some forms only, that it does not unite with everything and does not know everything. Similarly, I find that the sensitive soul is inferior in that respect to the rational soul. And as the actions of each of these substances belong to the same genus and are similar, I know that among them a substance more perfect and stronger is an active cause for a weaker and more imperfect substance, as has been said previously of the other substances.

Part VII

Master: You have understood it quite well. But what follows?

Pupil: It follows that all that is in the inferior substances is in the superior substances, but not that all that is in the superior substances is in the inferior substances. Thus growth and generation are in the animal soul, but sensation and locomotion are not in the vegetative soul, and sensation and locomotion are in the rational soul, while reason and knowledge are not in the animal soul. And I think that this principle is valid until the universal matter is reached and the universal form that envelops every form. It can thereby be seen that the more the substances are superior, the more forms they envelop, the more universal and comprehensive they are, until the universal primal matter is reached that supports all things.

Master: You must deepen your knowledge of the actions of these substances upon each other, according to the procedure used in this discussion.

Pupil: What do you mean?

Master: It is necessary, I repeat, for you to fix your attention on the demonstration of the existence of these substances, on the inquiry into the faculties of each of them, on the determination of their operations, on the comparison of the actions of each of these substances with the actions of the others, on the distinction of the impressions of these substances upon others, of their common characters and their differences, and all that is embraced by the types of logical questions relating to their investigation, so that what constitutes their similarity and their belonging to the same genus may be clear to you. You will then understand the action of some upon others and you will see the perfection of some in relation to the imperfection of others. And you must know that the knowledge of the simple substances and the intelligence of what is possible to understand about them are the greatest sense of repose and the greatest pleasure for the rational soul. And on the knowledge that the soul possesses of these substances, on its power to penetrate in them, on its perception of their forms and their properties, on its knowledge of their actions and their passions, depend for the soul the knowledge of the divinity and its union with it. Apply yourself therefore to the study of the simple substances and inspire yourself with the greatest zeal, particularly for what concerns the soul and the intelligence, for they possess all things and the forms of all things are in them.

Pupil: Since you have opened for me the gateway to knowledge of the simple substances and you have encouraged me to follow the path that leads to this knowledge, let us return to our discussion, I mean to the demonstration of matter and form in the intelligibles, as we did for the sensibles.

Master: When the existence of the intelligible substances is established, the existence of matter and form will be practically demonstrated to you. Linger then over the study of these substances and do not hurry, in your eagerness, toward that which follows, for on the knowledge that you will have of the existence of these substances, will depend your knowledge of what follows, and vice versa.

Pupil: The existence of these substances is to me a fact established by the method that consists in considering the different actions and that is founded on the belonging of these actions to the same genus and on their similarity. But I should like you to point out to me now, on the whole question of these substances, a general method to complete my knowledge of this subject.

Master: Consider the nearest of the sensible spheres and then in ascending order: you will find that the more the spheres rise, the greater their body, the more subtle their essence, the stronger their action, and the more simple their motion.

Pupil: I am considering this and I find it as you said.

Master: Also observe the motion of the universal body and observe the motions of all the spheres that are beneath it.

Pupil: I observe them and I find that they all move on account of the first motion with which the universal body moves.

Master: Regarding what you see of the motion of the universal body, has it its cause in the body or in some other thing?

Pupil: I think that the universal body finds in itself the cause of this motion.

Master: Is it possible that all the bodies that are beneath the universal body do not move by themselves, as you granted, while the universal body does move by itself?

Pupil: Why is it impossible?

Master: If it is possible, it may be that the essence of the universal body differs from the essence of the other bodies inferior to it.

Pupil: What proof is there that the essences of the bodies are a single essence?

Master: The proof is that they have motion in common.

Pupil: Do you think that the union of the superior spheres and of the inferior spheres in motion makes their common essence necessary?

Master: Note too their duration and their permanence, for in that they differ.

Pupil: If all bodies move on account of the motion of the universal body, why do the motions of these bodies differ in direction, while the motion of the universal body is one and has a single direction?

Master: It appears from this that the motion of the universal body is not by itself.

Pupil: How so?

Master: If its motion were by itself, the motion of the bodies that it moves could not differ from it in the direction of their motion.

Pupil: Do you think that by saying of the motion of the universal body that it is not by itself you are not constrained to say that everything mobile has a mover and so on to infinity?

Master: The proposition that everything mobile has a mover and so on to infinity is invalidated by the lack of mobility in the inferior extremity, by the fact that motion cannot be by itself, and that all motion cannot be the cause of motion.

Pupil: What will you say if, returning to the charge, I say that the motion of the universal body is by itself?

Master: I know the falsity of this assertion from what precedes. It is demonstrated still more conclusively by the diversity of the bodies in motion and existence and in the deprivation of motion.

Pupil: Add an explanation at this point.

Master: If the universal body moves by itself, it is necessary that it should be at the same time mover and mobile.

Pupil: How so?

Master: Because one of its parts cannot be motive only or mobile only.

Pupil: Why not?

Master: How can one of its parts be not mobile, when it is mobile by itself? For if it were mobile by itself, it would necessarily be entirely mobile and entirely motive: which is impossible.

Pupil: You have shown me that it would be inadmissible to say that the universal body is entirely mobile by itself.

Master: The result would also be that the motions of the parts of the body would not follow each other without the first motion pushing the second one and the passive object depending on the non-agent.

Pupil: Now I know in four ways that the universal body cannot move by itself. But is there still another way of demonstrating this?

Master: Yes, there is another way, besides those already shown: it is to consider that the heavens have a beginning and that they are not eternal.

Pupil: You have enlightened me. But if the heavens are not mobile by themselves, is it possible that they are moved without an intermediary by the First Mover?

Master: I did not believe that you could doubt that the heavens, that are the substance supporting the categories, are moved without an intermediary by the First Mover, after the logical proofs given according to the two methods that we have indicated for discovering the existence of the simple substances, that is, the method that consists in examining the properties of the First Author and those of the substance that supports the categories, and the method that consists in studying the impressions and the actions of these substances on others: since the substance that supports the categories comes from another essence from which it emanates. Understand from this that this substance does not emanate from the First Mover. Furthermore, I declare that if the dense unites with the subtle through an intermediary that agrees with these two extremes and if it receives its impression through an intermediary, as the human body receives the action of the rational soul through the intermediary of the animal spirit, as man receives intelligence through the intermediary of the rational soul, as the visual faculty unites with the bodies through the intermediary of the pupil and the subtle air, and as the universal soul unites with the bodies through the intermediary of the heavens that are a mean between the corporeal things and the spiritual things, similarly it is proved from this also that between the substance that supports the categories and the First Author there are also intermediary substances.

Pupil: I do not doubt, on the strength of the proofs that you have advanced, that there are substances intermediary between the substance that supports the categories and the First Author. But I should like you to increase my knowledge of the existence of these substances. Expand then the demonstration of this question.

Master: Do you not assert that some sensibles are superior to others and that the superior sensible is above the inferior?

Pupil: Why should I not?

Master: What is the cause of this?

Pupil: The cause is the difference between the inferior and the superior. And that is why it is impossible that the first should be in the rank of the second.

Master: Do you not assert also that the intelligible substance is higher and more subtle than the sensible substance?

Pupil: I do not say otherwise.

Master: Do you not also assert that some intelligible substances are higher and more subtle than others?

Pupil: Why is that necessary?

Master: For the reason that makes some sensibles higher and more subtle than others.

Pupil: What follows from this?

Master: The following reasoning results from this: If some sensible bodies are more noble than others, and if the superior body is more noble than the inferior, it is necessary that the highest of the superior beings should be the most noble and the strongest and that the last of the inferior beings should be the most worthless.

Pupil: It must be so.

Master: Therefore between the superior extremity of the sensibles and the superior extremity of the intelligibles, there is the same relation as between the inferior extremity of the sensibles and the inferior extremity of the intelligibles. Understand by this the existence of the simple substances, intermediary between the First Author and the substance that supports the categories.

Pupil: The existence of the simple substances is henceforth demonstrated by the methods that you acquainted me with. But a doubt on the matter still perplexes me when I consider our proposition that the forms borne by the substance that supports the categories are impressed by the simple substances and come from them. I see that the reason is disposed to understand this and that the proofs adduced previously on this question allow it to admit it, for these forms are accidents and nothing prevents them from coming from the simple substances and being united with them, as the sun's light emanates from the sun and unites with bodies. But how can one say that some simple substances emanate from others and that the essence of the substance supporting the categories emanates from the simple substance that follows it hierarchically?

Master: The essences of the simple substances do not flow at all, but it is their energies and their rays that flow and spread. For the essences of each of these substances are finite and limited and not extended to infinity, while their rays emanate from them and cross their boundaries and their limits on account of the subordination of these substances to the first emanation that proceeds from the Will. Just as the light that, from the sun, is diffused in the air—for this light transcends the limits of the sun and extends through the air, while the sun in itself does not go outside its limits—and just as the animal power flows from the rational faculty, whose abode is the brain, in the sinews and the muscles—for this power penetrates and spreads in all parts of the body, while in itself the substance of the soul does not spread and does not extend—so every simple substance extends its ray and its light and spreads them on that which is inferior, although the substance retains its rank and does not cross its boundaries.

Pupil: So, according to your statement, it is necessary that whatever emanates from the simple substances should be energies and qualities and not substances themselves.

Master: I shall show you that the rays that emanate from each of the substances do not exclude the concept of substantiality, although they are energies since they emanate from them. I assert that it is necessary that the cause should be more worthy of the concept of substantiality than the effect. And since this is so, it is necessary that all the light that streams from the superior toward the inferior should not be really and completely worthy of the concept of substantiality in relation to the first substance that is its cause. And from this viewpoint we may say of these substances that they differ in perfection from the point of view of substantiality. Therefore the superior substance among them is more worthy of the concept of substantiality than the inferior one.

But although the inferior is not equal to the superior in the concept of substantiality, it still does not exclude the concept of substantiality, for there emanates from the superior an energy that is a substance for that which emanates from it. Therefore the inferior substance is, in one sense, an energy for the superior substance from which it emanates, and, in another sense, it is a substance for the virtue that emanates from it. That is why nothing prevents substance from emanating from substance, when the substance from which it emanates is a simple substance.

Pupil: Explain this in more detail.

Master: It is axiomatic that whatever emanates from something belongs to the same genus as that from which it emanates, although both differ in disposition. And as the simple substance is a substance that communicates, it is necessary that what emanates from it should be a substance, although these two substances differ in disposition. Moreover, as the thing does not communicate for the reason that it is an accident, nothing prevents substance from emanating from substance. Now the proof that the emanation does not come from the fact that the thing that is communicated is an accident, is that a thing may be an accident without being communicated. This shows that the cause of the emanation is the subtlety of the light and the energy. Moreover, since the accidents communicate their essences although they are weaker than the substances, it is all the more reason for the substances to communicate their essences. Moreover, the cause that prevents bodies from emanating from bodies is that quantity, by reason of its dense and limited nature, is opposed to substance communicating its essence. Now as the simple substances are exempt from quantity, nothing prevents substances from emanating from them. Moreover, the energies and the accidents that emanate from substances, as light, heat, and other similar things, emanate from the energies and the accidents that these substances have, and not from the essences of these substances. Which proves that everything that emanates is similar to that from which it emanates and that only what resembles a thing emanates from it. It is therefore necessary that from the simple substances there should emanate a thing that is similar to it, that is, a simple substance. Moreover, if the superior substances did not give their essences to the inferior substances, they would not give them their names and their definitions. But they do give them their names and their definitions. Therefore they give them their essences. Now since the superior substances give their essences to the inferior substances and their essences are substances, it is evident that the essences of the inferior substances come from the essences of the superior substances. Moreover, as forms emanate from forms, so substances emanate from substances.

Pupil: Since it is said of the soul that it emanates from the intelligence, show me whether it is outside the essence of the intelligence or in the interior of its essence. For if it is outside the essence of the intelligence, it does not emanate from it. If on the other hand it is in the interior of the essence of the intelligence, there is no difference between them.

Master: The soul issues from the essence of the intelligence as power issues from a strong thing and does not enter its essence. But the fact that it issues horn its essence does not prevent it from emanating from it, for whatever emanates from a thing issues from the thing from which it emanates and withdraws from it on so emanating. Thus the soul emanates from the intelligence and issues from the essence of the intelligence on emanating from it: and the fact that the soul issues from the intelligence as power issues from a strong object does not prevent the soul from being a substance, for the thing that emanates from the intelligence is a substance in itself, although it is an accident in this respect that it emanates from another substance.

Pupil: Since some of the simple substances emanate from others, observe that the higher ones among them must diminish in themselves since the lower ones emanate from them.

Master: Since the inferior substances emanate from the essences of the superior substances as power issues from a strong thing, and not as essence issues from essence, it is necessary that the essences of the superior substances should not diminish in giving birth to the inferior substances. Similarly, it is necessary that these energies, I mean the inferior substances, should not separate from the essences of the superior substances, although they emanate from them. Thus the heat of fire does not diminish and does not leave it, although the fire produces heat in the air that is around it, and this heat is not that of the fire, for the fire can be withdrawn while the heat remains in the air: moreover, the two things are different and the heat that the air receives differs in power from that which is in the fire. Similarly, when the light of the sun spreads over the earth, the light that is borne by the essence of the sun is not diminished, although the first light emanates from it, and the light that spreads over the earth is not the light itself that the essence of the sun has. The proof of this is the difference of the subjects and the difference of the lights in power and weakness.

Pupil: Now I know that the energies that emanate from each of the simple substances, although they are the energies and the rays of the substance from which they emanate are still substances, and limited ones, on account of their virtue in themselves and because other energies emanate from them. The doubt that I entertained in this respect is gone. But explain something that comes to my mind, although it does not concern the present question. I find that the more the simple substances descend, the thicker and denser they become, until they become corporeal and finite. I find that the same thing happens with compound substances. I find, lastly, that the action of the divers substances on others is not equally evident. How then is it possible that the divine virtue should become weakened, transformed, and materialized, and that the action of the holy First Author should be more manifest in certain substances than in others, when the divine virtue is the highest degree of virtue, achievement, and perfection of all power and all majesty?

Master: It is impossible that the divine virtue should become weakened, but in the desire that attracts them toward it, the virtues rise and cast a shadow on what is below.

Pupil: Why is this so?

Master: Because every virtue that emanates from a thing is strong around it. It is therefore necessary that the virtue that emanates from the holy First Author should be stronger near him, in proportion as it is in his proximity, than it is elsewhere and far from him.

Pupil: This difference harmonizes with the virtue of a thing if this virtue is not essential to the thing: more so, if it is finite. Now the essential virtue of the First Author is infinite. Therefore it is impossible that this virtue should be stronger near him than it is at a distance. Now this is what I do not understand: How is it possible that something should recede from or approach an infinite thing, that is not enclosed in space, but that is equally in everything as everything is in it?

Master: It is true that the essential virtue of the holy First Author is not finite. But the increase and the diminution that constitute the differences between the forms do not introduce any difference in the efficient virtue in itself and do not make it finite.

Pupil: Why not?

Master: Because the form is received from the efficient virtue in the matter according to the aptitude of the matter in this respect, for if the matter were ready to receive a single form, perfect and without difference, the virtue would not fail to produce it.

Pupil: Why then did you say that the virtue emanating from the First Author is stronger near him, in proportion to his proximity?

Master: Beware of letting the difference of the virtue fall on the essence of the virtue, but attribute it to the essence of the thing that receives its action.

Pupil: How so?

Master: Since the matter that is nearer the source of the virtue is more ready to receive its action than the matter that is more distant, it is necessary that the virtue in the nearer matter should display more strength than in the more distant matter. Besides, this doctrine is not germane to the present question: it is contained in the science of the Will.

Pupil: All that has been said to establish the existence of the simple substances is sufficient. But summarize your talk and give me a résumé of the meaning of this question.

Master: If you want to envisage the whole, rise from the inferior to the superior. You will see the more subtle, more simple, stronger and more united being, whether matter as regards matter, form as regards form, motion as regards motion. And take the evidence as proof of what is obscure, the compound as proof of the simple, and the effect as proof of the cause, for if you succeed in this, you will attain the goal of your investigation.

Pupil: You have satisfied me on that point. But how can I imagine the order of these substances and their existence in each other?

Master: You must always take the sensible things as images of the intelligibles: then it will be easy for you to picture the intelligible things.

Pupil: What image shall I take from the order of the intelligible substances?

Master: Take as an image the absolute universal body, and that because the inferior is the image of the superior. For if you consider the composition of the absolute body and the order of its parts, the knowledge of the order of the simple substances will be easy for you.

Pupil: Point out to me the terms of the parallelism that there is between the simple substances and the sorts of the universal body.

Master: Place the primal matter opposite the substance that has all the forms of the body, for the matter has all the forms. Place the substance of the intelligence opposite quantity, for the intelligence, having two virtues, is subject to division. Arrange the substance of the soul opposite the figure that encloses quantity. And arrange the substance of nature opposite color, which is the last of the parts of the body, as nature is the last of the simple substances: besides, all color comes from nature. Just as the more the sight penetrates color on reaching the figure, quantity, and substance, the more does the being darken for it and hide on account of its subtlety: and just as the more it returns and leaves the substance for quantity, quantity for figure, and figure for color, the more does the being become perceptible to it from the fact of its density, so the more the intelligence penetrates that which is after the substance with categories, that is, the spiritual substance, until the primal matter is reached that corresponds to the substance, the more does the being on account of its subtlety darken for it and hide. And inversely, as it leaves the matter and returns toward a nearer substance, the being on account of its density becomes alight and more perceptible. The comparison that I make will facilitate your knowledge of the order and the different degrees of the spiritual substances.

And in general when you want to imagine these substances, the manner in which your essence spreads therein and comprehends them, you must raise your intelligence to the supreme intelligible, strip it and purify it of every stain of the sensible, deliver it from the prison of nature, and attain by the virtue of the intelligence to the highest knowledge that you can achieve of the truth of the intelligible substance, until you are as it were divested of the sensible substance and are in this respect so to speak in a state of ignorance. Then you will enclose in some fashion the entire corporeal world in your essence and you will set it as if in a niche of your soul. When you have done this you will understand the pettiness of the sensible in relation to the grandeur of the intelligible. And the spiritual substances will stand ready within your reach: set before you, you will see them envelop and dominate you, and it will seem to you that your own essence becomes one with these substances. And presently you will think that you are some part of these substances, on account of your connection with the corporeal substance. Then again you will think that you are the entirety of these substances and that there is no difference between them and yourself, on account of the union of your essence with their essences and the conjunction of your form with their forms.

Pupil: I do what you bid me, I rise according to the degrees of the intelligible substances and I stroll in their pleasant gardens. I find the sensible bodies in comparison with the intelligible substances extremely low and extremely imperfect and I see the corporeal world entirely swimming in them like a boat in the sea and a fledgling in the air.

Master: You have observed well and understood well. But if you rise to the universal primal matter and if you are illuminated by its shadow, you will then see that which surpasses all admiration: apply yourself therefore zealously to this, for it is in sight of this that the human soul exists and there is a great joy therein and perfect happiness.

Pupil: Teach me if the energies of these substances are finite or infinite. If they are finite, how do they proceed from an infinite virtue? And if they are infinite, how does something finite come from them into existence?

Master: The fact is, the Will, that is, the virtue that produces these substances, is finite according to its effect and infinite according to its essence. In these circumstances, its effect is finite. The Will is finite according to its effect because its action has a beginning and that is why it follows the Will. And it is infinite according to its essence, because it has no beginning. Inversely, we must say of the substance of the intelligence that it has a beginning, since it is an effect, and that it is infinite because it is simple and timeless.

Pupil: May heaven shower you with blessings! Show me how to imagine the union of the spiritual substances with the corporeal substances and the union of the spiritual substances with each other.

Master: Observe the union of light with the air, the soul with the body, the intelligence with the soul, and the union of the parts of the body with each other, that is, figure color, quantity, and substance, and their arrangement. And consider from this that the union of the accident with the body, of the accident with the soul, and of the soul with the body is proof of the union of the spiritual substances with each other. There is another proof in the fact that the union increases as the body becomes more subtle.

Pupil: I have often heard philosophers call these spiritual substances circles or spheres. Now it is clear that the figure of the circle is peculiar to the body only.

Master: Do not be surprised at this, for if they have called these substances circles and spheres, it is because some are superior to others and some envelop others.

Pupil: What am I to understand by this superiority and this envelopment?

Master: Just like your understanding of the sustaining in regard to the sustained, and of the cause as regards the caused and of the one knowing in regard to the known.

Pupil: Can we find in the particular substances proof of this envelopment that would allow us to judge the universal substances?

Master: Consider the virtue of nature: you will find that it envelops the body because it acts in it and the body is passive in regard to it and is clothed with it. Consider also the vegetative soul: you will find that it acts on nature and dominates it and you will find that nature is enveloped by it and experiences its action. Consider likewise the intelligence and the rational soul: you will find that both of them contain all the substances that are beneath them, that they know them, penetrate and dominate them, and particularly the substance of the intelligence, on account of its subtlety and its perfection. From these particular substances, you will conclude that some universal substances contain others and that all of them contain the compound substance in the sense that the soul contains the body and that the intelligence contains the soul. For the inferior substance among them is contained in the superior substance because the latter possesses and knows it. And the universal soul bears the corporeal world in its entirety, imagines and sees all that is in it, as our particular souls possess our bodies, imagine and see all that is in them: and still more the universal intelligence, by reason of its perfection, its faculty to extend, and the nobility of its substance. You will understand thereby how the First Author, sublime and holy, knows all things and how all things exist in his knowledge. And know this: Just as the essence and the form of the corporeal substance correspond to the essence and the form of the spiritual substance, so the envelopment by the spiritual substance corresponds to the envelopment by the corporeal substances, since the inferior is the image of the superior, as you have often heard it said. In these circumstances, it is evident that the envelopment of the corporeal substance by the spiritual substance indicates that the corporeal substance exists in it and that it is contained in it as all bodies exist in the body of heaven and are contained in it: and the turning of the spiritual substance upon itself in eternity and in permanent duration is like the turning of heaven upon itself by displacement and revolution.

Pupil: Add an explanation to this.

Master: If you will imagine the structure of the whole, that is, the universal body and the spiritual substances that contain it, consider the formation of man and take it as an image. For the body of man corresponds to the universal body and the spiritual substances that move it correspond to the universal substances that move the universal body, and among these spiritual substances the inferior substance obeys the superior substance and is submissive to it, until the motion reaches the substance of the intelligence. You will then find that the intelligence orders and dominates these substances and you will find that all the substances that move the body of man follow the intelligence and obey it while it perceives them and judges them.

Pupil: You have revealed a great mystery to me and a profound principle by telling me that the inferior motion of the universal substances has its cause in the motion of the substances that are superior to them: and that for this reason the inferior substances are submissive to the superior substances and obey them, until the motion reaches the highest substance. We thus find that all substances are submissive to the highest substance, that they obey it, that they follow it and that they move at its command. And I consider that the order of the particular soul imitates the disposition of the universal world.

If the present discussion had no other result but that, it would be sufficient, for it contains in itself the concept of the universal action and the passivity that are the ultimate end of wisdom.

Master: You have understood well what I have said in realizing that the inferior substances are submissive to the superior substances. Know too that this is the path that leads to perfect happiness and that allows us to obtain true delight that is our end.

Pupil: You have just proved to me in this third book the existence of the intelligible substances that no one but you has been able to demonstrate. I have acquired the knowledge of these substances, that nobody but myself acquires, according to my ability, and I have thus begun the study of this question. But let us consider in the fourth book matter and form, since that is our object, and demonstrate your previous thesis, namely, that there are matter and form in the intelligibles as in the sensibles.

BIBLIOGRAPHY

Asin Palacious, Miguel. Abenmassara y su escuela. Origenes de la filosofia hispano-musulmana. Madrid, 1914.

Brunner, Fernand. La Source de Vie. Livre III. Paris: Vrin, 1950.

Castro, Federico de. La Fuente de la vida, traducida en la siglo xii por Juan Hispano y Domingo Gonzales del arabe al latin, y ahora por primera vez al castellano por Federico de Castro y Fernandez. 2 volumes. Madrid. n.d.

Guttmann, Jacob. Die Philosophie des Salomon ibn Gabirol. Göttingen, 1889.

Kaufmann, David. Studien über Salomon ibn Gabirol. Budapest, 1899.

Millas Vallicrosa, José M. Selomo ibn Gabirol como poeta y filosofo. Madrid-Barcelona, 1945.

Text Edition: Fons Vitae ex arabico in latinum translatus ab Johanne Hispano et Dominico Gundissalino. Ex codicibus Parisinis, Amploniano, Columbino primum edidit Clemens Bäumker. Monasterii, 1892-1895.

ABOUT THE AUTHOR

Solomon ibn Gabirol (1021-1070) was an 11th century Andalusian poet who was born in Malaga and died in Valencia. He is credited as being a Jewish philosopher with, it is said, a 'Neo-Platonic' bent. He published over a hundred poems, as well as works of biblical exegesis, philosophy, ethics and satire. One legend credits Ibn Gabirol with creating a golem, possibly female, for household chores. In the 19th century it was discovered that medieval translators had Latinised Gabirol's name to Avicebron and had translated his work on Jewish Neo-Platonic philosophy into a Latin form.

Solomon ibn Gabirol is now best known for his work *Fons Vitae* ('Fountain of Life') and for his philosophical doctrine that all things, including soul and intellect, are composed of matter and form, and for his emphasis on Divine Will.

ABOUT THE PUBLISHER

Azafran Books was established with a clear aim in mind – to make available a selection of classic books for today's contemporary readers. The books in our catalogue have been selected from a broad range of themes; such as philosophy (occidental & oriental), mysticism & magic, new thought, religion & spirituality, folktales, mythology, cult fiction, poetry, social commentary, and psychology. Yet they all have a common theme, or purpose – to stimulate our thinking and modes of perception. For this reason, they have been chosen to be re-published and re-presented to the modern reader. Azafran Books have been re-edited, formatted, and presented with new design work – they are NOT scanned copies with original errors. Our books have been carefully re-published to the highest of standards – by a team of dedicated real people – not an algorithm! Our aim at Azafran Books is to bring a range of stimulating books, many of them largely forgotten, to the attention of the reader today. In other words, to bring you 'Classic Books for a Contemporary World.'

Please visit our website – www.azafranbooks.com

10105604R00079

Printed in Great Britain
by Amazon